A

CLASH OF KINGDOMS

DISCOVERY GUIDE

That the World May Know® with Ray Vander Laan

Volume 1: Promised Land
Volume 2: Prophets and Kings
Volume 3: Life and Ministry of the Messiah
Volume 4: Death and Resurrection of the Messiah
Volume 5: Early Church
Volume 6: In the Dust of the Rabbi
Volume 7: Walk as Jesus Walked
Volume 8: God Heard Their Cry
Volume 9: Fire on the Mountain
Volume 10: With All Your Heart
Volume 11: The Path to the Cross
Volume 12: Walking with God in the Desert
Volume 13: Israel's Mission
Volume 14: The Mission of Jesus
Volume 15: A Clash of Kingdoms

A
CLASH OF
KINGDOMS

—— 5 LESSONS ON ——

Paul Proclaims Jesus as Lord—Part 1

DISCOVERY GUIDE

**EXPERIENCE THE BIBLE IN
HISTORICAL CONTEXT™**
Ray Vander Laan
With Stephen and Amanda Sorenson

ZONDERVAN

A Clash of Kingdoms Discovery Guide
Copyright © 2017 by Ray Vander Laan

This title is also available as a Zondervan ebook.

Requests for information should be addressed to:
Zondervan, *3900 Sparks Dr. SE, Grand Rapids, Michigan 49546*

Focus on the Family and the accompanying logo and design are federally registered trademarks of Focus on the Family, 8605 Explorer Drive, Colorado Springs, Colorado 80920.

That the World May Know and Faith Lessons are trademarks of Focus on the Family.

ISBN 978-0-310-08573-7

All maps created by International Mapping.

All photos and artwork are courtesy of Ray Vander Laan, Paul Murphy, and Grooters Productions.

Cover design: Zondervan
Cover photography: Grooters Productions
Interior design: Denise Froehlich

First Printing April 2017 / Printed in the United States of America

CONTENTS

Introduction / 7

The Apostle Paul: A Timeline for His Life and Ministry / 16

Session One
    The Gospel of Caesar / 19

Session Two
    The Believers / 63

Session Three
    The Powers of Darkness / 109

Session Four
    The Philippian Jailer / 151

Session Five
    Confronting the Empire / 201

Notes / 247

Acknowledgments / 257

Bibliography / 261

INTRODUCTION

As a Bible teacher and study tour leader, I have had the privilege of hiking with thousands of Jesus followers in the lands of the Bible where Abraham, Ruth, David, Jesus, and Paul lived. It has been thrilling to watch group after group experience the pilgrim excitement of walking in the same places where Bible characters walked and to realize that their stories were set in real times and places. Many have returned home from places such as the wilderness of the Negev desert, the ancient streets of Jerusalem, the springs of En Gedi, and the villages of Galilee with a greater hunger for God's Word.

Seeing firsthand the context in which God revealed his redemptive plan has led them to a deeper faith and understanding of God's story. It has helped them to apply God's Word to their lives. Often they have said, "I will never read the Bible the same way again." I know their experience, for that has been my journey too.

Unfortunately, I made an assumption about understanding the Bible that turned out to be completely wrong. I knew it was helpful to study and understand the Hebrew Bible and the life of Jesus in the context of where and when particular events occurred, but I assumed that Paul, the great teacher who traveled throughout the Roman Empire, was more like a philosopher who spoke in the abstract with little awareness of the context of his audience. Then I visited the world that he was so passionate about—Ephesus, Philippi, Corinth, Athens, and Rome. And I discovered that the same experience of context that is helpful for understanding the Hebrew Bible applied to Paul's part of God's story too.

Although God's revelation is timeless and relevant to people throughout history, that revelation takes place in a cultural context—the unique circumstances and conditions—in which his people lived. Abraham cut up animals to seal a blood covenant much as the ancient Hittites did. The design of the temple of the Lord built by Solomon in Jerusalem was familiar to the neighboring cultures of

God's people. In Corinth where people displayed clay and marble body parts as votive offerings to the pagan god of healing, Paul described the community of faith as a body made up of many parts.[1]

God had a unique purpose for communicating his message through these culturally familiar concepts and practices that made the point of his message strikingly clear and relevant. Thus the cultural setting in which he placed his revelation is useful for not merely knowing what words mean but for understanding the message and application of the Text, much like the study of the language of ancient culture provides for the interpreter.[2] By learning how to think and approach life as the people of the Bible did, modern Christians will deepen their appreciation of God's Word.

Like the biblical writers before him, Paul communicated through the context of his world—its metaphors, manner of communication, historic events, and cultural practices—to address its problems and issues. The more we know about his world, the more clearly his teaching and letters speak to us in our cultural setting. For that reason, we begin our exploration of Paul's second teaching journey on the ancient *Via Egnatia* in modern Greece.

Paul's Second Teaching Tour: The Province of Macedonia

One of the highlights of my exploration of Paul's world was to follow the ancient trade route called the *Via Egnatia*, knowing that Paul had walked that very road. The ancient road is still visible and in some places is in remarkably good condition. Built more than a century before Paul brought the "good news" of the Messiah to the land of Greece in about 50 AD, the *Via Egnatia* represented the world of Imperial Rome. You can follow it west from Kavala (Neapolis in Paul's day) ten miles or so to the ruins of Philippi where it passes through the heart of the ancient city. That experience made a significant impression on my faith walk, not simply because I walked where Paul walked but because the road represented the confrontation of worldviews that had such a great impact on that part of the world and Paul's ministry to its people.

Although Christians traditionally have referred to Paul's travels as "missionary" journeys, the Bible does not use that language. Paul is Jewish, so it is more likely he viewed himself as a teacher (rabbi) making disciples rather than a missionary making "converts" in the sense that Christians use the word. His mission was to present Jesus as Savior and Lord and to invite people to believe in him and accept God's reign in their lives. In fact, the Text uses the word *convert* as often for Gentiles who join the Jews as it does for pagans who become Christians, and it is not used to describe Jews who follow Jesus. Because the early followers of Jesus were a branch of Judaism, Jews would not have thought they were changing religions when they recognized Jesus as Messiah.

Hence, to retain a Jewish flavor and communicate more clearly to a contemporary audience, I prefer to say that this study follows Paul on his second teaching journey,[3] which took him to the Roman province of Macedonia that we know as Greece. There, the gospel of Jesus confronted Hellenism, the worldview of Greek culture. These perspectives are diametrically opposed to one another and have been in conflict from the moment Satan took the form of a serpent and enticed our human ancestors with the forbidden fruit of Hellenism, which at its heart represents the choice to "do what seems good to you" rather than to obey the commands of God the Creator. Paul would discover that the fruit of that encounter continued to entice people in the Roman province of Macedonia.

In the cities of Philippi, Thessalonica, and Corinth the "good news" of Imperial Rome declared the emperor to be lord and god, the one who brought peace through Roman victory. How, then, would Paul's declaration that Jesus was Messiah, Lord, and Savior sound to "Roman" ears? He was not simply presenting another god to add to the deities of the Roman pantheon. Roman emperors claimed to be divine and were referred to as "son of god," "deified one," "savior of the world," and were addressed as "lord." Roman authors and poets declared this. Inscriptions on coins, altars, statues, and temples declared this. Everywhere the results of "divine" Caesar were seen in paved roads, running water, theaters, arenas, and temples. Paul's declaration that Jesus had come as Savior, Lord, and King would imply that the ubiquitous gospel of the Emperor could not be true. While he rarely confronted the kingdom of this world directly, the implications of Paul's message were clear, and the conflict between the gospel of Rome and the gospel of Jesus would be evident immediately.

Philippi was a Roman colony when Paul visited there. It was located on the *Via Egnatia*, the main road joining Rome to its provinces on the eastern end of the empire. Its strategic location had brought significant conflict to the region long before he arrived. The army of Cassius and Brutus, the assassins of Julius Caesar, brought their legions from the east and dug into the city and hill of the acropolis. There they prepared for attack by the army of Mark Antony and Octavian that marched to the scene from the west and camped outside the city on the Plain of Drama. Would Rome be a democracy? Or an empire? The question was answered in Philippi when the army of Antony and Octavian triumphed.

Octavian later defeated his ally Antony and became the Roman emperor, the divine son of a deified Caesar. The "golden age" of Roman peace had begun—as it always did, in blood—and spread throughout the Mediterranean world. Its "gospel"[4] (the word *gospel* was actually used) declared that peace came by devotion to the Roman gods and victory in war. *Pax Romana,* as they called it, was defined by prosperity (for some) and the pleasure and comfort of aqueducts, paved roads, theaters and arenas, and the games. For Roman citizens, at least in Rome and its colonies, peace provided daily bread as well. With that peace came the ironclad worldview that declared Caesar to be the divine son of god, lord of all, and the savior of the Roman world.

As I walked down the road I could imagine Paul, directed by the vision he had while still in Asia, walking from the east on the same paved stones. Accompanied by a few friends,[5] he brought the good news of a different kingdom. He brought peace—

shalom he would have called it—accomplished by the authority and sacrifice of Messiah Jesus, Lord and Savior of the world. This peace was not defined by economic prosperity but by a restored friendship with God and others. It did not come by victory in war, but by *grace* through the victory of the sacrificial death of Jesus who had been executed by Imperial Rome.[6] For me, the walk on the *Via Egnatia* brought the confrontation of the two gospels into focus. There were two sons of God, two lords, two kingdoms, and two definitions of peace—and they both took the *Via Egnatia* into the city of Philippi.

God's Great Plan of Redemption

Paul's visit to Philippi and other cities in Macedonia was one more step in God's plan to redeem his sinbroken world. For more than a millennium God had worked in partnership with people—Abraham and Sarah, Moses and the Hebrews, Rahab, Ruth, David, Elijah, Isaiah, and so many others—whom he called to be his witnesses to display the good news of his mercy to the world around them. He had entrusted his partners with his revelation and his presence. He had entrusted them with the Promised Land to provide for their daily bread and to give them a platform on the *Via Maris*—another trade route that served as the crossroads of the ancient world—from which to display him, so that people would come to know him and accept his reign in their lives.

Wherever God reigned in the hearts and lives of his people, his kingdom would come and *shalom* would replace the chaos brought into the world through sin. Yet chaos still reigned in the world. Had God's plan failed? Was Paul's message a new way to come to know God and to participate in his peace?

The answer is no. Although God's people experienced many failures in carrying out their mission, they were not failures. God used them to prepare for the next step in his great plan to redeem and restore his broken world: the coming of Jesus, God's Son. Jesus came to fulfill a mission he alone could accomplish.

His atoning death and resurrection are the only source of restored relationship with our Creator. God entrusted to his Son the very mission he had given Israel: to be the light of the world and make God's name known.[7] He revealed perfectly in word and action that God was creator of all, owner of all, and ruler of all.

Before his ascension and enthronement at God's right hand, Jesus entrusted the same mission God had given Israel—the same mission he came to fulfill—to his followers. Like Israel, followers of Jesus were to be his kingdom of priests who would put God on display and demonstrate his true nature, his great love, and his desire for all people to join his kingdom. They too would extend God's reign by doing his will so that his kingdom would come on earth as it already existed in heaven. They would be the light of the world, hallow his name, and make disciples by teaching others to imitate them as they imitated him.[8] They would become God's "word in flesh," demonstrating by their lives as well as their message the nature of the kingdom of heaven.[9]

So Paul and his friends walked into the Hellenistic cities of Macedonia—the Roman colony of Philippi, the provincial capital of Thessalonica, Corinth, and others—with the good news that God's reign was expanding and that his presence would live among those who believed the message. We will immerse ourselves in the history and culture of the Roman world in Greece as we seek to experience the story of Paul's visit. We will discover the stories of new believers—some Jewish and some Gentile—such as Lydia, the Philippian jail keeper, Aquila and Priscilla, Erastus, Jason, Dionysus, Damaris, and Crispus. We will see how they became living witnesses of the kingdom of heaven who put God on display in a very pagan, broken culture.

At every point, those of us who have been redeemed by the blood of Jesus will be challenged to take our place, like those who have gone before us, as God's partners in that same mission. God has called and empowered us to make known by our words and actions the good news of the redeeming power of Jesus. We must join the mission. Never has there been a greater opportunity to be God's coworkers[10] who mediate his presence as a kingdom of priests and make him known to a world in darkness.

I hope the example of Paul in the Roman world of Macedonia will encourage us to engage our culture as a minority,[11] seeking the welfare of the culture in which God places us. We do not have to be powerful or a majority! The early church in the world of Imperial Rome had a dramatic effect by being a faithful minority committed to carrying out their mission to a broken world. So we must be as well.[12]

Paul: Rabbi to the Gentiles

I have heard Paul described as the first "rabbi to the Gentiles," and I like that title. It captures his commitment to the Torah as well as his God-given mission to take the good news of Messiah to people who were not Jews: the very mission God gave to Israel. In the same way God had prepared Moses before him, God uniquely prepared Paul for exactly the task he called him to accomplish—being the Jewish messenger to the Gentiles who would take the message of the kingdom of heaven to the Roman world.

Paul was born about the same time as Jesus in the city of Tarsus (near the border of Turkey and Syria today), a wealthy commercial hub also known for a university equal to those in Athens and Alexandria. So for a time Paul's family lived in the social context of the wealth and philosophy—to say nothing of the morality—of the Roman world. His family experienced the rare privilege of being Roman citizens, but they were also Jews who belonged to the movement most devoted to living a righteous life in obedience to Torah—the Pharisees.[13]

When he was quite young, the family moved to Jerusalem where he experienced life in the Torah world of Jerusalem.[14] There he studied with Gamaliel, a highly respected expert on the Torah who became known as the greatest of all Jewish sages. His influence greatly shaped Paul's teaching. In fact, tradition records that Gamaliel taught Greek wisdom so that his disciples could interpret and apply the Torah to critique the philosophy and morality of the pagan, Hellenistic worldview that dominated Roman culture. So Paul was born in the Greek world of Tarsus and brought up in the Yeshiva of Gamaliel in Jerusalem. Plus, he was a Jew and a freeborn Roman. That combination doesn't happen by accident! Like Moses, Paul grew up without any idea of how God would use him in his plan, yet he was completely prepared in every way. The stories of Paul and Moses give great encouragement to those who become God's partners in mission.

In his own walk of faith, Paul was intensely passionate about the Torah and its application. He vehemently opposed those who interpreted it differently from the tradition he believed. That zeal—whether triggered by a particular teaching of the early followers of Jesus that he strongly objected to or the idea of opening the kingdom of God to Gentiles who had not converted to Judaism—likely played a part in Paul's persecution of the early church. But then, when Paul was on his way to Damascus in about 34 AD, he met Jesus.

Whatever else changed as a result of that encounter—his view of God's kingdom, his view of the nature of Messiah, his understanding of Jesus, his view of the Gentiles—Paul's life mission changed. He discovered that the long-awaited Messiah had come, and the mission of being God's kingdom of priests—displaying God in words and actions—was to extend to all nations and all people. In a sense Paul became the "Moses" to the Gentiles—a rabbi through whom God spoke in action and in word to lead people out of their bondage to the pagan worldview of Imperial Rome and into the gospel of Jesus and the *shalom* of the kingdom of God.

No longer would Paul's sole focus be on seeking to influence the Jewish people to faithfully live out the mission God had given them at Mount Sinai. God would use Paul, a brilliant scholar of Torah, a man who had been trained in Greek thought and who knew every biblical reason to keep the unclean Gentiles out of God's kingdom, to bring the message of God's redemption to the Gentiles! No longer would Paul fight for God's kingdom by exerting the power of this world. He devoted himself to follow the example of Jesus, the suffering servant, who sacrificed himself for the benefit of all who would believe.

When Paul met Jesus, he did not renounce his Jewish faith or allegiance to the Hebrew Bible. In fact, he took pride in being Jewish—circumcised on the eighth day, fluent in Hebrew, and a Pharisee of Pharisees.[15] But his understanding of God's plan of redemption changed. It was the same Bible, the same mission to the nations, the same kingdom of priests and kingdom of heaven. But the *way* God's kingdom would come had changed radically in his thinking. He realized that Jesus was the Messiah, the kingdom of God was at hand, and it came not by military conquest or deliverance but as a result of the redemptive suffering of Jesus.

Paul's journey through the great Roman cities of Macedonia shows his commitment to God's calling on his life as a continuation of the mission God gave to Israel. Through his story we will see the Hellenistic world of the first century and the Imperial theology of a Roman colony. We will discover the exhilarating power of the kingdom of heaven in the midst of great conflict. We will thrill with God's continued desire to restore *shalom* to all things and be amazed by how he continues to use the small and the weak to bring about his great plan of redemption.

As we join Paul in his context, we should find great hope for ourselves as we continue to partner with God in the same mission his people have always had. The increasing Hellenism of our own culture will not defeat us no matter how pervasive and powerful it appears to be. Rather, as Paul wrote from a Roman prison, I pray that we will "become more confident in the Lord and dare all the more to proclaim the gospel without fear."[16] As citizens of heaven, may we live "in a manner worthy of the gospel of Christ."[17] Our mission, like Paul's, is not simply to proclaim the great commission but to step into our role as partners in God's great plan of redemption for his people from Genesis to Revelation.

THE APOSTLE PAUL: A TIMELINE FOR HIS LIFE AND MINISTRY[1]

Birth and Rabbinic Training

6 BC Birth of Jesus (Luke 2).

5–6 BC Saul born in Tarsus in Cilicia to Jewish parents of the Pharisee tradition who were Roman citizens.[2]

4 BC Family moves to Jerusalem where he was brought up (Acts 22:3).

6–30 AD Studies "at the feet of" Gamaliel, one of the great Jewish sages (Acts 22:3).[3]

24 AD Jesus begins teaching (Luke 3:23).

27–28 AD Jesus' crucifixion, resurrection, and ascension (Luke 22–24).

Damascus Road

30–34 AD Saul persecutes followers of Jesus (Acts 5–7, 9).

34 AD Meets Jesus on the road to Damascus (Acts 9; Galatians 1).

35–38 AD Further preparation and training in Damascus, Arabia, Syria, Cilicia, and Jerusalem (Acts 9, 26; Galatians 1).

38–45 AD In Tarsus.

43 AD Peter is arrested, James is executed.

44–45 AD Is discipled by Barnabas (Acts 9, 11).

First Teaching Journey

46–48 AD First teaching journey begins in Cyprus. Changes name to Paul. Goes to Antioch of Pisidia, Iconium, Lystra, Derbe (Acts 13–14).

49 AD Emperor Claudius expels Jews from Rome.

49 AD Jerusalem Council (Acts 15). Probably writes Galatians.

Second Teaching Journey

50 AD Travels from Tarsus to Galatia, but Spirit would not let him go to Asia, Mysia, Bithynia. In Troas receives vision of man from Macedonia (Acts 16).

50 AD	Goes to Macedonia: Philippi, Thessalonica, Berea, Athens (Acts 16–17).
51–52 AD	In Corinth with Aquila and Priscilla for eighteen months (Acts 18).
52 AD	Returns to Jerusalem; visits Ephesus, Antioch, Galatia (Acts 18). Probably writes 1–2 Thessalonians.

Third Teaching Journey

| *54–57 AD* | In Ephesus (Acts 19). Probably writes 1–2 Corinthians, Romans. |
| *57 AD* | In Troas, Macedonia, Achaia for three months (Acts 20). Then in Corinth for winter. Heads back to Jerusalem for Pentecost, traveling through Macedonia—Thessalonica, Philippi—and on to Troas and Miletus where he meets with the Ephesian elders (Acts 20). |

Arrest in Jerusalem

| *57 AD* | Arrest in Jerusalem (Acts 21–23). |
| *57–59 AD* | Imprisoned in Caesarea; has audiences with Herod Agrippa, Festus, Felix (Acts 23–26). |

"Fourth" Teaching Journey

| *59–61 AD* | Travels toward Rome; is shipwrecked and spends winter on Malta. A prisoner in Rome for two years but continued writing and teaching (Acts 27–28). Probably writes Ephesians, Colossians, Philemon, Philippians. |
| *62–64 AD* | Apparently released from prison and may have traveled to Crete, Colossae, Ephesus, Philippi, Spain, Corinth, Miletus,[4] and probably writes 1 Timothy and Titus. |

Martyrdom

| *65–68 AD* | Arrested, possibly in Asia Minor, and returned to Rome. This is based on church tradition with no biblical references. Probably writes 2 Timothy. Martyred during Nero's persecution, traditionally by beheading, which was the penalty for a Roman citizen. |

THE GOSPEL OF CAESAR

I love walking on the *Via Egnatia*, the ancient Roman Road that stretched nearly 650 miles from Byzantium (the European side of modern Istanbul) in the east to Dyrrhacium (Durres in present-day Albania) in the west, where it connected via the Adriatic Sea to the Appian Way in Italy. The large paving stones that Roman soldiers placed almost 200 years before Paul walked on the *Via Egnatia* are still in remarkably good repair. As I walk a section of this ancient road between Neapolis (Kavala today) and Philippi, I find myself surrounded by the silence of a pine forest—quite isolated from the bustling, modern world of northern Greece and the tour buses that pass nearby. Step by step I hear the sound of my sandals on the stones, and it feels as if I have traveled back in time to the world of Paul. I imagine what it might have been like to walk with him as he journeyed from the Roman province of Asia into Macedonia to share the gospel of Jesus Christ, Savior and Lord of all.

As I walk that narrow, ancient road, I wonder what Paul thought about as he walked.

Did he recall his experience on another road—the Damascus Road—where the resurrected Jesus met him as he urgently pursued the early followers of Jesus so that he might arrest and punish them? That encounter radically changed Paul's understanding of Jesus the Messiah and his life's calling.

Did he consider the importance of Macedonia to the Greek, and now Roman, empires? Did he ponder its Hellenistic, human-centered worldview that was so antithetical to that of his own Jewish training in the teachings of the Torah?

Did he anticipate how his journey was bringing him ever closer to the heart of Imperial Rome and the emperor who claimed to be the Son of God and declared that he had brought peace to all?

Whether such thoughts occupied his mind is impossible for us to know. But we do know that Paul had studied the Torah (the Text, God's Word) extensively and understood it to be the summary of God's great story of redemption. He knew that God chose the Hebrew people to be his partners in bringing the message of redemption to a world in chaos because of sin. At Mount Sinai, God assigned to his people a task of utmost importance: to be a light to the Gentiles and make God's name known to all nations so that all people would be blessed and the whole earth would be filled with the knowledge of God, liberated from bondage to sin, and join the hosts of heaven in praising him.[1]

Paul not only understood the mission God gave to his people at Mount Sinai, he recognized that Jesus, the promised Messiah, had carried out that mission and commissioned all of his followers to continue it by bringing the good news—the gospel—of his coming to the ends of the earth. Thus Paul's calling was to announce the arrival of the Messiah who died to redeem all of humanity from bondage to sin, and afterward rose again and ascended to be seated at God's right hand as the true Son of God, Savior, King, and Lord of all. In fervent, but humble, obedience to Jesus, Paul pursued the mission to be God's light to the Gentiles by living a righteous life that would invite others to know and give glory to God.

In his brilliant defense before governor Festus, Paul described his calling in those very terms:

> *But God has helped me to this very day; so I stand here and testify to small and great alike. I am saying nothing beyond what the prophets and Moses said would happen—that the Messiah would suffer and, as the first to rise from the dead, would bring the message of light to his own people and to the Gentiles.*

> **Acts 26:22–23**

Eager to fulfill his God-given mission, Paul entered the Roman colony of Philippi. Despite the fact that an opposing gospel ruled the hearts and minds of the Philippians, he began sharing the gospel of Jesus.

Opening Thoughts (3 minutes)

The Very Words of God

> *After Paul had seen the vision, we got ready at once to leave for Macedonia, concluding that God had called us to preach the gospel to them.*
>
> *From Troas we put out to sea and sailed straight for Samothrace, and the next day we went on to Neapolis. From there we traveled to Philippi, a Roman colony and the leading city of that district of Macedonia.*
>
> **Acts 16:10–12**

Think About It

There can be no more life-changing event than to accept God's free gift of redemption and submit ourselves to his reign in our lives. The Bible makes it clear that being a follower of Jesus makes us partners with God in his great story of redemption and restoration. As his partners, God gives us the mission of making him known to all people. But when we submit ourselves to his lordship and pursue what we believe that mission to be, what do we expect will happen?

What are our expectations for how our service for Christ will be received?

How do we respond when we think we are supposed to do one thing but the doors keep closing?

How easy or difficult do we anticipate accomplishing our mission will be, and what keeps us motivated to pursue it when we face obstacles?

Video Notes (32 minutes)

God's great story

Paul proclaims the gospel of Christ to people who live by the gospel of Rome

The *Via Egnatia*: Paul's route into Macedonia

Philippi: battles that changed the world

The emperor establishes his claim as lord and god

Heroon: built to honor and deify the most accomplished heroes

Jesus: exalted to the highest place by being a humble servant

Video Discussion (6 minutes)

1. How aware were you that in the Roman Empire there was an existing gospel—the gospel of Caesar, the deified emperor—that conflicted with the gospel of Jesus Christ?

What was the gospel of Caesar, and what insight does it give you into what Paul and the early Christian community faced as they sought to obey Jesus' command to take his gospel to the ends of the earth?

How does being aware of conflicting gospel(s) affect the way we might approach sharing the gospel in our culture?

2. The battles that took place on the Plain of Drama near Philippi literally changed the course of world history. What impact did those battles have on the beliefs and lifestyle of the people who lived in Philippi, which Octavian (Caesar Augustus) designated as a Roman colony?

3. If you had grown up in Philippi, immersed in a culture that sought honor for oneself above all else and at any cost, how do you think you would have responded to the gospel message of Jesus that Paul and Silas brought to town?

4. Paul was on his second teaching journey, visiting churches he had established previously in Asia Minor, when he had a vision that he interpreted to mean that God wanted him to go to Macedonia. Eager to fulfill his God-given mission to tell the world of God's plan of redemption, he immediately headed to Philippi, a major city in Macedonia, which we know of as northern Greece.

   On the map of Paul's second teaching journey, locate Philippi and trace Paul's route from Troas to Neapolis, where he headed west on the *Via Egnatia*. Also consider Philippi's strategic location and the role of the *Via Egnatia* in the battles of 44 BC that effectively ended Rome as a republic and ensured its future as an imperial power.

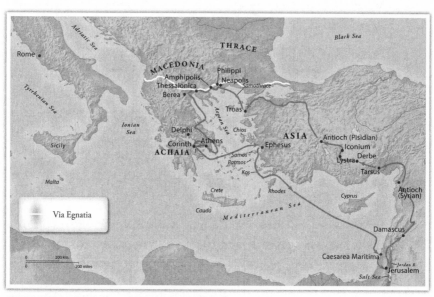

PAUL'S SECOND TEACHING JOURNEY

Small Group Bible Discovery and Discussion (14 minutes)

Paul Brings the Gospel of Christ to Philippi

Philippi was established on a hill above the Plain of Drama in about 360 BC and was soon ruled by Phillip II of Macedonia, father of Alexander the Great. Gold and silver from the mines of Mount Pangaion above the city are believed to have financed the military campaigns of both Phillip II and Alexander the Great that spread the worldview and self-serving lifestyle of Hellenism throughout the known world. More significant, Philippi's close proximity to two ancient seaports and its location on the *Via Egnatia* made it vitally important commercially and militarily. The city served the Greek objectives well and later played a strategic role in the expansion of the Roman Empire.

In 42 BC, about two years after the assassination of Julius Caesar, one of the most far-reaching battles in Roman history was fought on the Plain of Drama, just beyond the city walls of Philippi. The battle changed the course of Western civilization. On one side, Octavian and Anthony envisioned Rome as an empire ruled by an emperor. On the other, Cassius and Brutus wanted to restore Rome as a republic. Octavian and Anthony were victorious, putting into motion what would become Imperial Roman rule by a deified emperor.

Octavian, the adopted son and heir of Julius Caesar who would become known as Caesar Augustus, then designated Philippi as a Roman colony.[2] He populated it with soldiers from the legions he defeated on the Plain of Drama (and later veterans of other Roman legions) who would influence the local culture and demonstrate the advantages of the Roman way. As citizens of a Roman colony, they enjoyed all the benefits and privileges of citizens of Rome, and those privileges were highly regarded and protected.

By the time Paul arrived in Philippi in 50 AD, the city had become like a miniature Rome. Luke refers to it in the book of

THE PLAIN OF DRAMA AS SEEN FROM THE ANCIENT CITY OF PHILIPPI

Acts as the "leading city of that district" (Acts 16:12). As in all Roman colonies, temples for the worship of Greek, Egyptian, and local gods were permitted as were Jewish synagogues, but the worship of Roman gods and the emperor as lord and god was predominant. In fact, the imperial temple dominated one side of the forum in Philippi, and historic references include mention of an altar of Augustus.

So when Paul came, a powerful gospel message was being lived out in Philippi—the gospel of Caesar, the deified savior and lord who brought peace and prosperity to those who served him well. What would happen when Paul brought a different gospel to the forum of Philippi—the good news of redemption for all people through the shed blood and resurrection of Jesus, the true Son of God? Certainly, the stage was set for confrontation between two "sons of god," two "lords," and two "saviors" representing two opposing kingdoms—the kingdom of heaven and the kingdom of this world.

1. Paul came to Philippi with a mission—the same mission God gave to Israel at Mount Sinai, the same mission Jesus fulfilled by his life and ministry, and the same mission Jesus gave to his followers who would come after him. That mission is to be a light to the world and represent God in such a way that all the world will come to know him.

   a. What do you learn from the following passages about the nature of the mission God has given to all of his people and the impact he wants them to have on the world around them? (See Exodus 19:3–6; Isaiah 12:4–6; 42:6; 43:10–12; 49:6; Matthew 5:14–16; 28:18–20.)

   b. From what you have learned about the Roman colony of Philippi, what potential conflicts do you see occurring as Paul seeks to fulfill his mission there?

> ## FOR GREATER UNDERSTANDING
> ### What Is a Kingdom of Priests?
>
> The Bible uses the concept of a priesthood to describe the mission God has given to his people (Exodus 19:3–6). In ancient times, priests would mediate between the gods and the people. A priest represented and acted on behalf of the god; so, in a sense, to observe the priest was to know the god.
>
> At Mount Sinai, God gave his people the mission of being his "priests" to the whole world. The nature of that mission is for God's people to serve him and humanity by demonstrating through their words and actions God's will and character. God's people are not only to *bring* the message but to *be* the message in everything they do.
>
> In what we know as the "Great Commission" (Matthew 28:18–20), Jesus extended this mission to all of his followers. Thus the apostle Peter reminds followers of Jesus that they are "a royal priesthood" (1 Peter 2:9, 12). For this reason, God has called and commissioned all redeemed followers of Jesus to this day to make him known to the whole earth and to live good lives that are worthy of that calling—the same mission God gave to the Hebrews at Mount Sinai.

2. When Paul came to Philippi in 50 AD, he came to a Roman colony where the Roman way was put on display. So the city already had a gospel—the gospel of Caesar as lord, god, and savior—that brought peace and prosperity to its citizens. As a result, the citizens of Philippi were devoted to Roman privilege and law as the way to peace and a good life. Let's consider how the gospel of Jesus challenged the fundamental claims of the gospel of Caesar. Read Philippians 2:5–11 and then consider the contrasts between the two gospels.

    a. Caesar Augustus claimed a miraculous birth that made him a descendant of the Roman gods Venus and Apollo. Furthermore, he was the adopted son of Julius Caesar who was deified following his death, making

Augustus the deified son of a god. What does the Bible say about Jesus and his divinity? (See Mark 1:1–3; Luke 2:11; Philippians 2:5–8.)

What is ironic about Jesus' claim to deity when compared to that of Caesar Augustus?

b. Caesar Augustus became "lord" by political action, military victory, and official decree. Many thousands sacrificed their lives in battle so that he could gain power and recognition for himself. The divine right to rule that Caesar Augustus claimed for himself was confirmed by the authority and dominance he wielded. In contrast, what was Jesus willing to sacrifice for the benefit of others, and why did that make him worthy in the eyes of God? (See Philippians 2:6–11.)

Explain how the attitude and actions of Jesus that God deemed worthy of recognition and honor were opposite those held by Caesar and the community of Philippi.

Even though there is no indication that Paul overtly critiqued Caesar Augustus or labeled his claims to be lord and god as fraudulent, what impact do you think his presentation of the news about Jesus might have had on people in Philippi?

DATA FILE
Octavian Becomes "Lord" and "Savior"

After Octavian crushed the republican resistance to Rome becoming an empire in 42 BC and later defeated Antony in 31 BC, the way was clear for him to seize power in Rome. But in a surprising move, he actually forgave some of his enemies, returned power to the Roman Senate, and relinquished control over his armies. In response, the Roman Senate granted him the title "Augustus," meaning the honored or worshiped one!

The title "Augustus" conveyed power far beyond political power, giving Octavian absolute authority over humanity and nature. Gradually he accumulated all the political powers of an emperor. After Julius Caesar's spirit was declared to be enthroned in heaven with the gods (deified), as affirmed by a bright comet that appeared during his memorial, Octavian began to accept honor as the son of a deified one. Thus Caesar Augustus became the worshiped son of a deified one, or the son of god!

Then Augustus came to be viewed as savior because he saved the Roman republic from the disaster of constant civil war. And finally peace, the *Pax Romana*, came as a result of his reign. No wonder there was conflict when Paul brought the good news of Jesus—the true Son of God, the Lord and Savior who offers peace to all who believe—to Philippi.

c. At the beginning of the video presentation, we saw
    the Roman gate of the city of Jerash, which testified
    to the gospel of a later Roman emperor, Hadrian. The
    gospel of Caesar claimed to be a gospel of peace and
    security—the *Pax Romana*. It brought running water,
    paved streets, temples, fountains, baths, education,
    theaters, art, the games, recognition of accomplish-
    ment, accumulation, and other things that made life
    pleasant and happy (at least for the upper classes). A
    Roman emperor who brought an end to wars and ush-
    ered in such peace, which Caesar Augustus did, was
    viewed as lord, god, and savior of the world.

    In contrast to the Roman peace, Paul preached the
    gospel of the Savior who brought peace by restoring
    God's *shalom*—harmony, meaning, purpose, beau-
    ty, and wholeness—to a world suffering under the
    chaos of sin. Read Acts 10:34–38, John 14:27, and
    Philippians 1:1–2 and discuss specific differences
    between God's message of peace through Jesus Christ,
    Lord and Savior, and the peace Caesar offered. What
    thoughts and questions might the people of Philippi
    have had as they listened to Paul's message?

3. When Paul brought the good news of Jesus Christ to
    Philippi, it quickly became clear that he was not repre-
    senting the gospel of Caesar or advocating the Roman

idea of peace. What about the gospel of Christ seems to have caused great concern for the people of Philippi, and how did they respond? (See Acts 16:19–21.)

Faith Lesson (4 minutes)

For the most part, those of us who follow Jesus and live in Western cultures aren't radically different from other people in our communities. Christianity has always been a significant part of our cultural heritage. Although we may face opposition to our beliefs or slander, we generally do not face the severe persecution that Christians who live in some other cultures have endured (and endure to this day).

Ours is not the situation Paul faced in Philippi when he brought the gospel—the good news that Jesus Christ, the Son of God, the Lord, the Savior of the world had died and rose again so that all who submit to him could know true peace. Everyone who heard Paul's message already knew the gospel of *Pax Romana*—the Roman peace. Their son of god, lord, and savior who reigned supreme and brought the benefits of peace was Caesar. To even suggest that any other gospel existed was radical and dangerous.

For Paul to proclaim the gospel of Christ in Philippi was to imply that Caesar's gospel was a fraud. Would anyone believe Paul? Would he survive the reaction of those who realized that the gospel he proclaimed would turn their world upside down? As we continue this study, we will see that men and women, rich and poor, slave and free became convinced that Caesar wasn't really god and savior, and that what Rome called peace really wasn't. They too chose the radical gospel of Christ over that of Rome.

What does this have to do with us? We live in a culture that, like Rome, proclaims a gospel of its own making. All too easily we bow to the gospel of humanism, making ourselves our own Lord: "I am lord of my life; I decide what is right and wrong; I do it my way." We serve the gospel of hedonism by living for pleasure and leisure. We honor the gospel of materialism by making life all about what we have and what more we can get. And we worship as heroes those who make it to the top of the heap.

1. Just as God brought Paul to Philippi to share the radical news of the gospel of Christ, God has led each follower of Christ to this time and place so that we can continue the mission he gave to his people at Mount Sinai and bring by word and example the good news of Christ. The question is, are we willing to take our place in fulfilling the mission God has given?

    How willing are you to not only *bring* the message but *be* the message?

2. As followers of Jesus, we bring a radical message: the good news of the Son of God, Lord and Savior, who sacrificed himself to bring true peace—harmony with God, harmony with others, and to the best of our ability, harmony with all of creation. Words alone will not convince our broken world of the truth of the gospel of Christ. If we live a self-righteous, self-serving, self-absorbed, narcissistic lifestyle, we won't persuade anyone of the radical truth of the gospel—they already live this way. Many in Philippi became convinced that the gospel of Christ was true by what they heard and *saw* in Paul, Silas, Timothy, and Luke. It is no different for us.

By which gospel do you live? The gospel of this world or the gospel of the kingdom of heaven?

What needs to change in your heart, mind, and life so that people will come to know who God really is?

Closing (1 minute)

Read Philippians 1:1–6 aloud together: "To all God's holy people in Christ Jesus at Philippi, together with the overseers and deacons: Grace and peace to you from God our Father and the Lord Jesus Christ. I thank my God every time I remember you. In all my prayers for all of you, I always pray with joy because of your partnership in the gospel from the first day until now, being confident of this, that he who began a good work in you will carry it on to completion until the day of Christ Jesus."

Then pray, thanking God for giving us the true gospel, the good news that Jesus has come and sacrificed himself so that we can be restored to a relationship with God who gives peace to everyone who calls on him. Thank him for that great kingdom of priests he raised up and commissioned to be his partners in bringing and being the gospel message so that we could hear it and praise God for who he is. Ask him to help us to be faithful in carrying out that mission in our world. May we not live for ourselves, but empty ourselves as Jesus did and thereby complete the work of making the God of heaven known on earth!

Memorize

To all God's holy people in Christ Jesus at Philippi, together with the overseers and deacons: Grace and peace to you from God our Father and the Lord Jesus Christ.

I thank my God every time I remember you. In all my prayers for all of you, I always pray with joy because of your partnership in the gospel from the first day until now, being confident of this, that he who began a good work in you will carry it on to completion until the day of Christ Jesus.

Philippians 1:1–6

The Gospel of Christ Provokes Imperial Rome

In-Depth Personal Study Sessions

Study 1 | Heroes Worthy of Honor

The Very Words of God

> *The greatest among you will be your servant. For those who exalt themselves will be humbled, and those who humble themselves will be exalted.*
>
> **Matthew 23:11–12**

Bible Discovery

A Hero in the Roman World

In the Roman world, not everyone got to be a hero. The bar was set very high. A hero (or heroine) was either a demigod who had been born of one divine parent and one human parent or a person who, in the face of danger and adversity, displayed exceptional courage and self-sacrifice for the benefit of humanity. The hero also must have suffered during his or her life, struggled against death, and died sacrificially. Following the person's death, societies would organize and evaluate the evidence to determine whether the person had lived a life that was worthy of deification and veneration. If so, the person was given divine status in recognition of his or her extraordinary accomplishments.

Although designated heroes were worshiped, they were not divine in the same sense as gods such as Jupiter or Apollo. Even so, deified heroes such as Heracles, Achilles, and Alexander played an important role in Greek and Roman religion. Permanent altars and shrines were erected in their honor. They were feared, respected, venerated, and petitioned by those who worshiped them in the hope of receiving protection, prosperity, success, and fertility. Sacrifices, offerings, and libations were made in their honor. Worship of specific heroes included public processions, games, and festivals.

What would the Philippians think when Paul brought a message of a great hero—indeed, the very Son of God—who displayed his greatness through humility and sacrificial service to others?

DID YOU KNOW?
Gaining a Name Above All Others

In the context of his time, Paul's statement that God gave Jesus "the name that is above every name" (Philippians 2:9) meant more than we might realize. People of ancient times understood a name was more than just a label that identified a particular person. A person's name was significant because it also conveyed an understanding and knowledge of the person's character. A name expressed the essence of a person's reputation, honor, and authority.

Because Jesus humbled himself, submitted to God, and suffered on behalf of all sinners, God considered him to be worthy and rewarded him with a name—honor, reputation, authority—above all others. This was the opposite of how the Roman way worked. To the Romans, a person's name was exalted by climbing to the top of the pile for one's own benefit, and it didn't matter if others were harmed in the process. To be exalted was to have one's name on a heroon or to have one's statue in an imperial temple, and those honors weren't achieved through humility or self-sacrifice.

1. In Philippians 2:9, Paul explains that God exalted Jesus "to the highest place and gave him the name that is above every name." This meant that Jesus had a higher, more honorable name than Philip II or Caesar, whose names were inscribed around the city of Philippi! Even more remarkable, Jesus did not gain honor because he tried to elevate himself to a higher class as the Romans did; he did the opposite. Instead of claiming his rights of equality

with God and seeking the glory due him, he "made himself nothing" or "emptied himself" and became human so that he could be a servant to all!

To better understand the values of God's kingdom as demonstrated by Jesus, take note of what Jesus did that God deemed worthy of honor, worthy of the names "King of kings," "Savior," and "Lord of lords." Read Philippians 2:6–11 and compare Paul's description of Jesus in that passage to Isaiah's description of God's servant in Isaiah 52:13–15; 53:2–3, 12.[3] Feel free to highlight the common descriptions in these passages.

Isaiah 52:13–15 (NRSV)	Isaiah 53:2–3, 12 (NRSV)	Philippians 2:6–11 (NRSV)
See, my servant shall prosper; he shall be exalted and lifted up, and shall be very high. Just as there were many who were astonished at him—so marred was his appearance, beyond human semblance, and his form beyond that of mortals— so he shall startle many nations; kings shall shut their mouths because of him; for that which had not been told them they shall see, and that which they had not heard they shall contemplate.	For he grew up before him like a young plant, and like a root out of dry ground; he had no form or majesty that we should look at him, nothing in his appearance that we should desire him. He was despised and rejected by others; a man of suffering and acquainted with infirmity; and as one from whom others hide their faces he was despised, and we held him of no account. . . . Therefore I will allot him a portion with the great, and he shall divide the spoil with the strong; because he poured out himself to death, and was numbered with the transgressors; yet he bore the sin of many, and made intercession for the transgressors.	. . . though he was in the form of God, did not regard equality with God as something to be exploited, but emptied himself, taking the form of a slave, being born in human likeness. And being found in human form, he humbled himself and became obedient to the point of death—even death on a cross. Therefore God also highly exalted him and gave him the name that is above every name, so that at the name of Jesus every knee should bend, in heaven and on earth and under the earth, and every tongue should confess that Jesus Christ is Lord, to the glory of God the Father.

What do you notice from these passages about how God's servant gains honor?

How readily does the kingdom of this world recognize and value what God considers worthy of honor?

When those who pursue the honor offered by the kingdom of this world see the contrast to what God regards as worthy and how he bestows honor, what is their response? Why?

2. What do the following verses reveal about the difference between the values and lifestyle of people God honors and rewards as heroes versus the values and lifestyle of those who seek to be honored as heroes by this world?

   a. Matthew 6:1–4

    b. Matthew 23:1–12

    c. Mark 12:38–40

    d. Luke 14:11

3. Glory, honor, and peace as defined by Rome were highly valued and ruthlessly sought after in the Roman Empire. In a letter Paul wrote sometime after leaving Philippi, he emphasized how a person receives glory, honor, and peace in God's kingdom. Read Romans 2:6–11 and note the differences between the gospel of Christ and the gospel of Caesar.

What does this passage communicate about the gospel of Caesar and the peace offered by Rome?

How do you think people who had conducted their lives according to the value of the gospel of Caesar might have responded to the statement that God does not show favoritism (v. 11)?

FOR GREATER UNDERSTANDING
To Be Honored as Divine

On the north side of the agora (Greek) or forum (Roman) of Philippi are the ruins of a small temple called a heroon. Such shrines were normally erected over the tomb and interred bones of an ancient Greek or Roman hero and were used for the veneration or worship of that hero. Many examples can be found in or near ancient Greek and Roman cities.

Although scholars are not certain, the heroon of Philippi (see photo of steps and artist's rendering of the shrine) may have been dedicated to the worship of Philip II of Macedon, father of Alexander the Great. We know the Greeks recognized and honored Phillip II as a deified hero because of his leadership genius and military success that made the Greek Empire possible. We also know that a heroon was built for his veneration in the city of Aigai where he died.

The honors of a heroon would have greatly pleased Philip II, who thought of himself as one of the gods and arrogantly sought the honor of deification during his lifetime. His pursuit of such recognition may have cost him his life. During his daughter's wedding, the procession included statues of all twelve Greek gods in their finest splendor. But Philip II made an addition to the procession: a thirteenth statue—of himself—in equal splendor as if he were one of the gods![4] Not long afterward, he was killed by one of his own guards, possibly because of his efforts to proclaim his own deity.

THE STAIRS OF THE HEROON AT PHILIPPI (TOP). ARTIST'S SKETCH OF WHAT THE HEROON AT PHILIPPI MAY HAVE LOOKED LIKE (BOTTOM).

During the first century, heroes of the Roman Empire were honored and worshiped as being divine in the same way that Philip II was. Emperors also claimed to be divine, but in a different sense. No heroons dedicated to the worship of any emperors have been found, but this did not diminish their right to be honored and worshiped. It did not lessen the expectation of divine status that would be granted upon their death. Emperors often claimed divine status based on the deification of their deceased ancestors, and some even sought deification while they were alive. So imagine the impact that Paul's teaching about the deity of Jesus would have on a city named for Philip II, who was also worshiped as a deified one.

Reflection

It's all too easy for us to believe that the gospel of Caesar is simply ancient history that has nothing to do with us today. However, the Hellenistic values displayed by the gospel of Rome are very much alive in our world. That gospel still holds people in self-serving bondage to sin. And those of us who seek to follow Jesus today are not immune to its influence.

Paul went to Philippi with one mission: to proclaim and display the gospel of Christ so that other people would come to know God and follow Jesus Christ as Savior, Lord, and King. To people who lived under the influence of "lord" Caesar—where the heroon and the imperial temple declared the glory of human heroes who spent their lives trying to be divine—Paul explained that Jesus was the hero God honored above all others because he humbled himself and willingly suffered for others. Paul taught the Philippians who chose to follow Jesus to be faithful disciples who would declare and display the glory of God by having the same mindset as Jesus (Philippians 2:1–6). As followers of Jesus today, we have the same calling.

We live in a world that is still sold out to the gospel of Caesar—the values of Hellenism that advocate the selfish pursuit of one's own best interests, recognition of one's accomplishments, the acquisition of power and possessions, and pride in one's status. In order for us to turn that value system upside down and acknowledge Christ's lordship and display God's glory by seeking to be like Jesus in all that we do, what changes in character and priorities must we make?

Read Philippians 2:1–6, then write down practical ways you can display in your life the qualities Paul outlined for the Philippian believers.

In what ways do you think believing in Jesus Christ as Lord, accepting him as King, and submitting to his authority in every part of life is as foreign to the culture in which we live as Paul's message was to the Philippians who had known no gospel other than that of Caesar?

How willing are you—in your own "Philippi," where the values of Rome reign—to radically live out and proclaim the lordship of Jesus Christ?

Study 2 | Paul Pursues the Mission

The Very Words of God

> . . .*because of the grace God gave me to be a minister of Christ Jesus to the Gentiles. He gave me the priestly duty of proclaiming the gospel of God, so that the Gentiles might become an offering acceptable to God, sanctified by the Holy Spirit.*

> **Romans 15:15–16**

Bible Discovery

The Apostle Paul: Itinerant Rabbi to the Gentiles

Paul has been described as the first "rabbi to the Gentiles." That designation acknowledges Paul's faithful commitment to the Torah and his great passion to bring the gospel of Jesus to people who were not Jews. It also recognizes Paul's commitment to continue the mission God gave to Israel: to be a light to the Gentiles and to make God's name known to all nations. Paul pursued that mission as a teacher—a "rabbi" in the Jewish way of thinking—who traveled widely in order to present Jesus as Savior and Lord and invite all people to accept the reign of God in their lives and become disciples who lived as Jesus lived (1 John 2:6).

1. What do we know from the Text about Paul's training in the Torah and his commitment to obey God according to the practices of the Jewish faith? (See Acts 22:1–5; 26:4–5; Philippians 3:3–7.)

Considering Paul's background, how well had God prepared him for his ministry to the Gentiles?

2. At the time Paul met Jesus, he was zealously committed to his Jewish faith even to the point of defending God's name (meaning his character and reputation) by persecuting early followers of Jesus. From that perspective, how did Paul come to know that God had chosen him to be a rabbi who would testify that Jesus was Savior and Lord, and specifically that he was to fulfill that mission to the Gentiles? (See Acts 9:1–17; 26:12–18.)

How committed was Paul to carry out his God-given mission of preaching the gospel of Jesus? (See Acts 9:19–28; 26:19–20.)

How did he view his role as a Jew in fulfilling that mission to the Gentiles? (See Romans 15:8–19.)

DATA FILE
Paul, Itinerant Rabbi to the Gentile World

After meeting the resurrected Jesus on the Damascus Road, Paul accepted the same commission God gave to Paul's ancestors at Mount Sinai, the same commission Jesus gave to his disciples—to display him accurately to the world so that people of all nations would come to know him. In pursuit of this God-given mission, Paul lived out the message of *kiddush ha shem* (seeking to honor God and increase his reputation by everything he did) with a level of dedication and fervor rarely seen. Toward that end, he made three teaching journeys that are documented in the book of Acts. There is also a hint that he made a fourth teaching trip, although we know little or nothing about it from the Text.

On his first journey (Acts 13–14),[5] Saul (his name at the time) and Barnabas were sent out by the faith community of Antioch. They spent time in Cyprus, the homeland of Barnabas, where Sergius Paulus, the Roman proconsul, decided to follow Jesus. He is the first named believer of Saul's teaching and presumably the reason Saul began using the name *Paul.* From Cyprus, they

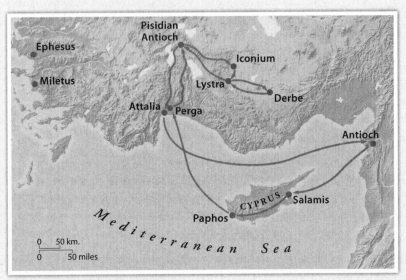

PAUL'S FIRST TEACHING JOURNEY

went to Antioch of Pisidia, the hometown of Sergius Paulus. Then they moved on to Iconium, Lystra, Derbe, and Perga. Finally, they returned to Antioch, retracing their steps to visit believers in the cities where they had taught.

On Paul's second teaching tour (Acts 15:36–18:22), he was accompanied by Silas, not Barnabas. They retraced the route of Paul's previous tour, stopping in all the cities where he had taught previously. They continued west, but the Spirit prevented Paul from going into the province of Asia or into Bithynia. Then, while in Troas, Paul had a vision of a man from Macedonia (Greece) pleading for help, which Paul took as God's leading to teach in that region. Immediately he sailed across the Aegean Sea to Neapolis, where he continued his journey on the *Via Egnatia* toward Philippi.

After establishing a community of believers in Philippi, Paul went on to Thessalonica, Berea, Athens, and Corinth, where he stayed for an extended period of time. When he left Corinth to return to Jerusalem, Paul stopped in Ephesus and left his coworkers Aquila and Priscilla there to continue teaching the gospel. After spending time with followers of Jesus in Jerusalem, Paul returned to Antioch, from where he started his third teaching tour (Acts 18:23–21:19).[6]

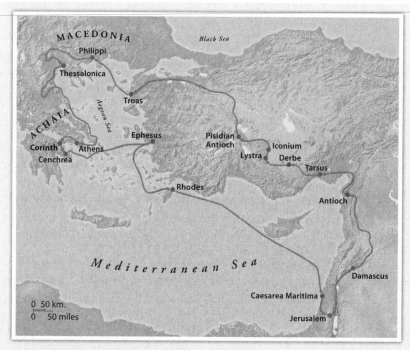

PAUL'S SECOND TEACHING JOURNEY

On his third teaching journey, Paul followed the interior road from Antioch to Ephesus, passing through the cities where he had established faith communities on his first tour. After spending more than two years in Ephesus, the commercial center for the entire province of Asia, he then visited believers in the cities of Greece where he had taught previously and sailed back to Troas. From there he sailed to Miletus where he met with leaders of the Ephesian believers, then sailed to Caesarea and walked to Jerusalem.

In Jerusalem, Paul was falsely accused and arrested. Because of threats to his life, he was imprisoned in Caesarea where he appealed his case to Caesar in Rome. So Paul's fourth and final teaching journey (Acts 22–28) began with a trip to a prison in Rome. While in prison, Paul continued to write and teach. He apparently was released for a time and may have traveled to Crete, Colossae, Ephesus, Philippi, Spain, Corinth, and Miletus. Tradition holds that Paul was again arrested in Asia and taken to Rome where he was beheaded—as was his right as a Roman citizen—during the persecutions of Emperor Nero.

3. When Paul began his second teaching journey in pursuit
    of his mission to teach the gospel and make God known,
    he retraced the route of his first teaching tour and visited
    the churches he had established in Galatia. He was eager
    to move on to new territory, but for a reason unknown
    to him, what happened—not once, but twice? (See Acts
    16:1–7.)

4. How did Paul respond to this unexpected circumstance?
    (See Acts 16:8–12.)

    What did Paul do when he felt he at last received leading
    from God?

    Do you think Paul had any idea what would result when
    he took the next step, or what the step after it would be?
    Why or why not?

What enables a follower of Jesus to faithfully take that next step into the unknown?

DATA FILE
How Paul Understood His Mission

Paul's Account of His Mission	Hebrew Bible Account of Israel's Mission
Acts 26:12–18	*Ezekiel 1:25–2:1*
Jesus appeared as a light brighter than sun	God appeared as brilliant light
Paul fell to the ground	Ezekiel fell face down
Jesus told Paul to "get up"	God told Ezekiel to "stand up"
Jesus spoke to Paul and gave a mission	God spoke to Ezekiel and gave a mission
Paul sent to Israel and Gentiles	Ezekiel sent to Israel
Galatians 1:13–16	*Isaiah 49:1–6*
Paul set apart from birth	God chose Isaiah before he was born
Paul sent to Israel and Gentiles	Isaiah to be light to Israel and Gentiles
Galatians 1:13–16	*Jeremiah 1:5*
Paul set apart from birth	Jeremiah set apart before conception
Paul sent to Israel and Gentiles	Jeremiah sent as prophet to Gentiles

---

Reflection

Like Paul, every follower of Jesus has been called to be a priest of God's kingdom who puts God on display by everything he or she does or says. In order to serve God passionately, we must be "all in" in our commitment to be in the place he desires— whether it's the college we choose, the career we pursue, where we decide to live, or what our family lifestyle will be. We need to make every significant life choice in light of how we demonstrate what God is like in that environment.

No matter how committed we are to the mission, none of us knows what lies ahead. We will, as Paul did, encounter obstacles to going where we believe God wants us to be. Paul demonstrated faithfulness by being willing to adjust his plans when God seemed to close the doors, even when it must have seemed strange to him. As he confronted obstacles, he kept trying different possibilities, all the while trusting God to determine the final destination by removing some possibilities and making new ones available.

So what will we do? How will we be faithful when we face unexpected obstacles in pursuing the mission Jesus has given to us? How will we respond when we find ourselves in a totally different place or situation than we thought Jesus wanted? Will we trust God to lead us when it's not where we think we should go?

Read Mark 6:45–56 and consider the unexpected lesson Jesus' disciples experienced as they obeyed Jesus and set off for a brief boat trip along the northern shore of the Sea of Galilee—from near Capernaum to Bethsaida.

> The disciples had just witnessed a great miracle, so they probably were excited when they launched their boat. But, despite their best efforts, what happened to the disciples, and how difficult was it for them?

> If you had been one of the disciples, what might you have thought about that experience and what Jesus wanted you to do?

Where did the disciples end up, and what happened when they got there? What do you think the disciples may have realized about following Jesus and understanding his leading?

As you consider what you have explored through this study, what have you realized about pursuing the mission Jesus has given you to make him known in your world?

What is your commitment to be a "partner" with God in that mission, and how much personal effort and sacrifice are you willing to put into the task?

What tests your faithfulness in pursuing the mission, and what is your commitment to taking that one next step into the "unknown"?

Study 3 | Paul Presents God's Formula for Peace

The Very Words of God

Peace I leave with you; my peace I give you. I do not give to you as the world gives. Do not let your hearts be troubled and do not be afraid.

John 14:27

Bible Discovery

Two Kingdoms Promise Peace

Philippi is an ideal place to consider the Roman concept of peace that Paul encountered as he shared the gospel of Jesus throughout the Roman Empire. After all, the Roman way to peace had unfolded before the Philippians' eyes. Its foundation was laid in 42 BC on the Plain of Drama outside Philippi when Octavian, soon to become Caesar Augustus, defeated the assassins of his adoptive father, Julius Caesar. That battle ushered in the golden age of *Pax Romana*, an accomplishment that helped to earn Octavian the title of "savior" because he brought peace and public safety to the Roman Empire. Ironically, Octavian expressed his gratitude for the victory that brought his brand of peace by building a temple to war and vengeance—Mars Ultor, Mars the Avenger—in the forum in Rome.

So what would happen when Paul came to Philippi bearing news of the kingdom of God and its promise of peace when the kingdom of Rome had already established what it called peace? What would happen when Paul claimed that Jesus the Messiah, Lord and Savior, had sacrificed his own life to bring peace to the whole world when Caesar had slaughtered and conquered in order to bring peace? What formula for peace would Paul advocate, and what would people see and understand when he presented the gospel of Jesus to them?

1. The peace of Rome was obtained through brutality and domination and maintained by power and privilege. In contrast, what does the Text reveal about the source and nature of God's peace? (See Psalm 4:8; 29:11; 128:5–6; John 14:27; Acts 10:36; Galatians 5:19–24.)

What does the Text say about the peace the world offers—epitomized by *Pax Romana*—and those who pursue it? (See Psalm 53:3–4; Isaiah 48:22; 57:21; 59:8; Romans 3:10–18.)

DID YOU KNOW?
Shalom, God's Answer to the Pax Romana
The Hebrew understanding of peace, or *shalom*, can be defined as any condition that is exactly as God intended it to be. Peace is God's creation before sin entered the picture. It is harmony between God and his creation, God and humanity, and between people. *Shalom* is life without hate, prejudice, envy, violence, injustice, disease, disaster, and death. It is life with meaning, purpose, beauty, and wholeness—without imperfection. It is the essence of who God is and satisfies the longings of every human heart.

2. The *Pax Romana* was built on domination, pride, and the spoils of war that brought comfort, pleasure, and safety to the Roman Empire. It enabled a privileged few to live a very "good life" at the expense of many. In contrast, what does living in peace look like for those who are followers of Jesus? (See Romans 12:18–21; 14:19; 2 Corinthians 13:11; 1 Timothy 2:1–2.)

    What evidence do we find that the early communities of Jesus followers understood the gospel message and had received the gift of God's peace? (See Acts 2:42–47; 3:1–10; 4:32–35; 5:12–16.)

3. Caesar Augustus wrote his own first-person account of his life and accomplishments, called *Res Gestae Divi Augusti* or *The Acts of Divine Augustus*,[7] which defined Roman peace. In contrast, Paul presented an entirely different formula for peace. Both perspectives are summarized in the chart on the next page.

The Acts of Divine Augustus	The Acts of the Apostles
Describes in three points how Augustus subjected the whole earth to the rule of Rome, ushering in Rome's golden age of peace. Written by Augustus and inscribed on bronze pillars in Rome.	Describes how God's kingdom of peace came through the shed blood of Jesus and is spread to the world by God's human ambassadors. Written by Luke.
First, Augustus reformed the priesthood and restored 82 temples and built more than a dozen more in order to renew the worship of traditional Roman gods.	First, peace comes only from God through Jesus, who shed his blood to reconcile all things and restore harmony with God. Peace is a result of what God has done, not what we seek to do.
Second, Augustus brought peace by leading the Roman legions to conquer and subjugate the entire earth. These conquests, in which thousands were killed or captured as slaves and cities were destroyed, brought (in his mind) an end to war and resulted in peace. The Roman peace brought glory and reward for some, suffering and struggle for others.	Second, peace does not come through the bloody effort of human conquest. Peace is not earned or deserved; it is not reserved for the rich, the powerful, or the wise. It is God's free gift for everyone—rich or poor, Jew or Gentile, slave or free.
Third, Augustus took credit for the prosperity the spoils of war brought to the Roman Empire. He built and rebuilt temples, roads, and public buildings, and funded public spectacles such as gladiatorial contests and the Olympic games.	Third, real peace is not dependent on material prosperity; it is not the same as comfort and enjoyment. While these benefits are a pleasant blessing, peace that truly satisfies has to do with finding harmony with God, with others, and with God's creation itself.

a. How would you describe the differences in the understanding and practice of peace between the kingdom of Caesar and the kingdom of God?

What about the peace of the gospel of Jesus do you think attracted or offended the people of Philippi, and why?

b. If you were to write a three-point description of what our culture considers peace to be, how would you describe it? First, how does peace come?

Second, who deserves or earns peace?

Third, what does peace look like?

4. The differences between the peace of the gospel of Caesar and the peace of the gospel of Jesus Christ did not go unnoticed. What kind of response did Paul receive when he presented the gospel message and sought to establish communities of Jesus followers wherever he went? (See Acts 14:1–7; 16:13–21; 17:1–8; 19:23–31.)

THINK ABOUT IT
Pax Romana: Peace for Some, Not for All

Following in the footsteps of Julius Caesar, who based his right to rule on the peace he brought to Rome through conquest, Caesar Augustus continued the push for Roman security and peace. To Caesar Augustus, *Pax Romana* not only meant the cessation of war, it meant Rome could use the resources of its conquered territories and people for its own benefit. The plunder of conquest made Rome the envy of nations, bringing security, economic prosperity, leisure, beauty, and the pleasures of life to Rome's wealthy and powerful.

But not everyone lauded the *Pax Romana.* Tacitus, the Roman historian, recounts the words of a conquered chieftain: "Robbers of the world, they have by their universal plunder exhausted the land. . . . If the enemy be rich, they are rapacious; if he be poor, they lust for dominion; neither the east nor the west has been able to satisfy them. To robbery, slaughter, plunder they give the lying name of empire; they make solitude and call it peace."[8]

His comments are not unlike those of Paul, who quotes several Old Testament passages in his Romans 3:10–18 description of those who do not know peace:

- "There is no one righteous, not even one; there is no one who understands; there is no one who seeks God. All have turned away, they have together become worthless; there is no one who does good, not even one."[9]

- "Their throats are open graves; their tongues practice deceit."[10]

- "The poison of vipers is on their lips."[11]

- "Their mouths are full of cursing and bitterness."[12]

- "Their feet are swift to shed blood; ruin and misery mark their ways, and the way of peace they do not know."[13]

- "There is no fear of God before their eyes."[14]

Reflection

Peace was highly valued—a coveted commodity—in the danger-ous, tumultuous world of the first century. That is one reason Caesar Augustus was considered divine: he had accomplished the impossible by bringing his gospel of peace, safety, and prosperity to the Roman Empire. So it shouldn't surprise us that Paul taught about peace. It was essential that followers of Jesus in the Roman Empire realize that God's peace—*shalom*—was far more than the absence of conflict or the ability to achieve happiness and com-fort in life.

In every letter of instruction in Christian living that Paul wrote to the churches he established on his teaching journeys, his greeting included blessings of "grace and peace from God." To the Philippians, Thessalonians, Corinthians, Ephesians, Colos-sians, Galatians, and Romans as well as to Timothy, Titus, and Philemon, Paul began by reminding them of the gift of grace and peace that comes from God to all those who believe. Further-more, his instructions to the communities of Jesus followers he had established frequently included reminders of how to demon-strate what God's peace—*shalom*—looked like. As a reminder of how foundational is the peace that comes from God, read the beginnings of Paul's letters (Romans 1:7; 1 Corinthians 1:3; 2 Cor-inthians 1:2; Galatians 1:3; Ephesians 1:2; Philippians 1:2; Colos-sians 1:2; 1 Thessalonians 1:1; 2 Thessalonians 1:2–3; 1 Timothy 1:2; 2 Timothy 1:2; Titus 1:4; Philemon 1:3).

> Each of these communities of Jesus followers (and individ-uals) faced challenges in living out the gospel of Christ, in bringing shalom to a world that pursued a different kind of peace. In what ways do you think being firmly rooted in God's grace and peace helped them to fulfill the mission to which God had called them?

How do you live differently when the peace of God is your foundation, the starting point for everything you do?

As followers of Jesus today, we also live in a Hellenistic world that pursues a different kind of peace from the peace God gives. Which obstacles, desires, or distractions of the world around you hinder you from experiencing the peace of Jesus in your life?

What hinders you from demonstrating shalom in the broken, suffering world in which you live?

THE BELIEVERS

At one time, I thought of Paul as the great missionary who traveled around the Roman Empire proclaiming the good news of salvation so that people would believe in Jesus and be saved. This certainly was the central theme Paul taught at every opportunity—to Jew and Gentile, pagan and God-fearer, slave and Roman citizen. But, and this is not to diminish our need for God's gift of salvation in any way, there is more to the gospel message than "Jesus saves." From the beginning, God's great message of salvation has been about redeeming and restoring *shalom*—the harmony, beauty, and perfection he originally created—to a world broken by sin. Thus the gospel message encompasses the redemptive sacrifice of Jesus, the restoration of God's creation, and the truth that God reigns over all![1]

Paul was trained by the best Jewish scholars and had a brilliant understanding of the Scriptures. He understood that God had called his people throughout history to be his witnesses, a light to the nations around them. They were to put God on display and make him known to people who did not know him. At Mount Sinai, God chose the Jewish people to be his partners— his kingdom of priests—in proclaiming by their words and demonstrating by their lives his message of redemption. They were not simply to *bring* God's message to a broken world; they were to *be* that message of redemption and restoration.

Fully committed to that mission, Paul took the gospel message to "the ends of the earth" at a level unknown until his day. He declared by word and example the good news that God's chosen Messiah—the King of Kings and Lord of Lords who reigns on high—had come to redeem and restore all things to himself. As was often the case during his teaching journeys, Paul did not stay in Philippi for long. He was there for only a few days. But Paul and his companions shared the gospel of redemption and restoration through Jesus, and people believed. They accepted God's reign in their lives, and God's kingdom was extended into Philippi!

Paul taught those who believed that they had a mission too: to become God's message, to be a community of people whose lives proclaimed that the Lord is taking charge and this is what it looks like! Whenever the gospel is lived out, it has a significant impact—a fact that followers of Jesus today would do well to remember. The small community of believers in Philippi, a city where Jewish influence had not been as strong as in some other locations, became a community deeply committed to living out what they believed. In fact, Paul's letter to the Philippian believers a few years after his initial visit with them was the most positive and complimentary of all the letters he wrote to the churches he established. Let's consider how the gospel of Christ was received in Philippi.

Opening Thoughts (3 minutes)

The Very Words of God

One of those listening was a woman from the city of Thyatira named Lydia, a dealer in purple cloth. She was a worshiper of God. The Lord opened her heart to respond to Paul's message. When she and the members of her household were baptized, she invited us to her home. "If you consider me a believer in the Lord," she said, "come and stay at my house." And she persuaded us.

Acts 16:14–15

Think About It

When we accept God's call to be a partner in his great story of redemption by sharing the gospel with people who don't know him, we can't be certain of what lies ahead or where that mission will lead us. The same was true for Paul when he walked into Philippi to share the good news of Jesus. He had never been to Philippi or met the people there. He didn't know what impact the gospel would have—if it would be received and believed or if it would be reviled and opposed. He didn't know who, if anyone, would believe. Yet he went to be a light to the Gentiles so that they could be set free from bondage to sin and be restored to God's family.

> In what ways do you think Paul was prepared to share the gospel in a community that was to a great extent unknown to him?

> What would you say is most important for us to understand, know, or do in order to be ready to share the gospel message of redemption and restoration with people in our world?

Video Notes (29 minutes)

The father's house, a picture of redemption

The good news comes to Philippi

A place of prayer

Lydia, the God-fearer

God's kingdom comes!

Citizens of a colony of heaven

"Contend" for the faith

Don't distort the message

Video Discussion (7 minutes)

1. In what ways does the picture of community in the family of God as presented in the video differ from your understanding or experience of Christian community?

    To what extent does our understanding of salvation—restoration to God's family—encompass the practical aspects of our daily lives and relationships?

2. Why do you think it is significant that Paul sought out "a place of prayer" in Philippi, a Roman colony?

How much of an impact does it appear the community of God's people in Philippi had before Paul arrived?

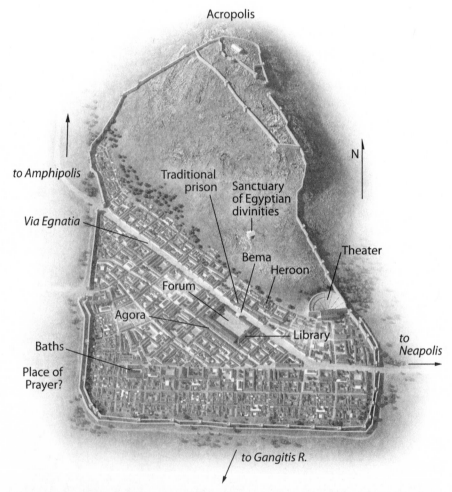

Acropolis

to Amphipolis

N

Via Egnatia

Traditional prison

Sanctuary of Egyptian divinities

Bema

Heroon

Theater

Forum

Agora

Library

to Neapolis

Baths

Place of Prayer?

to Gangitis R.

NOTICE THE "IMPORTANT" PLACES IN THE ROMAN COLONY OF PHILIPPI—THE *VIA EGNATIA*, THE THEATER WHERE GLADIATORIAL COMBAT TOOK PLACE, THE FORUM, THE PRISON. OUTSIDE THE CITY WALLS, SOMEWHERE NEAR A TRIBUTARY OF THE GANGITIS RIVER, WAS A PLACE OF PRAYER WHERE PHILIPPIANS WHO WORSHIPED GOD GATHERED.

3. When a person today accepts the gospel message that Jesus is Savior, Lord, and King, what do we expect will happen?

As we consider how Lydia responded to the gospel message, what might we be missing out on, in light of what restoration to God's family really means?

4. What message did Paul convey to the believers of Philippi about "contending" for the gospel, and why would this have been significant to them, given the history and culture of their city?

FOR GREATER UNDERSTANDING
What Is the Gospel?

Paul walked into the city of Philippi, a Roman colony, in 50 AD to bring the gospel of Jesus to people who did not know him. *Gospel* is the English translation of the Greek word *evangelion*, meaning "good news." Although we may think of *gospel* as primarily a religious word, the people of the Roman Empire knew of it as the term for good news about an emperor—news such as his coronation, a great accomplishment, or the birth of an heir.

Paul, of course, knew that this was what people in the Roman world understood *gospel* to mean. But he also was familiar with another meaning of *gospel*, or *good news*, from the Hebrew Bible. Notice how the prophet Isaiah uses *good news* in Isaiah 52:7:

> *How beautiful on the mountains are the feet of those who bring good news, who proclaim peace, who bring good tidings, who proclaim salvation, who say to Zion, "Your God reigns!"*

Try to imagine how this good news, the gospel of the God who reigns, who brings peace, and who proclaims salvation would be received by people who already had the gospel of their own emperor who demanded recognition, honor, and worship.

Small Group Bible Discovery and Discussion (16 minutes)

The Gospel Message of Redemption and Restoration

In God's great story of redemption, unfolded for us through the pages of the Bible, God is portrayed as the One who redeems and restores. He is deeply concerned for all of his children who suffer and are in bondage to sin. He is so concerned that to every person who accepts his gift of redemption he gives a mission: to be his partner in sharing the good news so that all people may experience redemption and be restored to the security and *shalom* of God's family. Faithfulness to that mission is why Paul brought the gospel message to Philippi.

Lydia, a woman who apparently worshiped God with the Jewish people in Philippi, heard Paul teach and became a follower of Jesus. Her story is one of the more dramatic examples of the power of God's Spirit anointing the work of Jesus' followers. Although Lydia is mentioned in only five verses in all of Scripture, the evidence her story provides of God's redeeming work through his human partners is inspiring. We see God's preparation for the gospel coming to Philippi and Paul's faithfulness to the mission. We see the power of God's Spirit at work in the human heart. We rejoice in Lydia's restoration to God's family and her immediate desire to participate in the mission God has given to everyone who follows Jesus.

1. The apostle Paul was a Pharisee and a rabbi who had been thoroughly trained in the Text by one of the most highly respected rabbis of his time. He was deeply committed to obeying God's commands in every way possible. He described himself as being born into the tribe of Benjamin, circumcised on the eighth day, zealous for God, and faultless in righteous living based on the Law of Moses.[2] He enthusiastically embraced Israel's mission to be a kingdom of priests who would display God's character to all people so that they would come to know him. And when Paul met the resurrected Jesus on the road to Damascus and recognized him as the Messiah, he embraced the mission of redemption as Jesus defined it for him. Read Exodus 19:3–6 to refresh your memory of the mission God gave to his people at Mount Sinai.

   a. What happened at Mount Sinai was a pivotal, defining moment for God's people. How does the mission that God gave his chosen partners there relate to the mission God has given all followers of Jesus? (See John 20:19–21; 1 Peter 2:9–10.)

   b. What specific mission did Paul receive following his encounter with Jesus on the road to Damascus? (See Acts 9:3–6, 15.)

c. Do you think this was a mission Paul expected to be given, one he found easy to pursue? Why or why not?

DID YOU KNOW?
Restored to God's Family

For followers of Jesus who live in contemporary Western cultures, the idea of being redeemed and restored to God's family sounds good, but perhaps not as compelling as it might be. If we are to grasp the full meaning of being restored to God's family, we need to go way back in biblical history—back to the ancient Middle East where life was centered around the extended family.

The extended family, or household, was thought of as the "father's house" or *beth ab*. It could easily comprise thirty or more family members from several generations: the head of the family (the patriarch), his wife (or wives), his younger brothers, unmarried children, and married sons with their families (a woman usually joined the *beth ab* of her husband). The job of the patriarch was to use the family resources, which he controlled, to ensure the protection and care of each family member.

If a family member lost connection to the *beth ab* due to capture by enemies, poverty, or bad choices, the patriarch was responsible to do whatever it took to restore that person to the safety and fellowship of the family. Anyone in that cultural setting who found himself or herself without connection to the *beth ab*, such as a widow or orphan, was at serious risk because he or she had no means of support or protection.

So when we read in the Text about God redeeming and restoring his lost children, this is the image we need to have in mind. God longs to restore every one of his children who has been lost through bondage to sin. He is the loving Father who longs to embrace his children in the security and blessing of his *beth ab*. And, as Abraham realized thousands of years ago, God wants his human partners to join him in the mission of putting him on display so that those who are estranged from him—even the most broken, lost, and hopeless children—can experience restoration and the faithful care of the *beth ab*.

2. The Hebrew Text is filled with images of God's love and compassion for his creation. We see evidence of his desire for all people outside his *beth ab* to be restored to the family of God. Read the following passages and describe what you discover about (1) God's character, love, and compassion, and (2) the mission God gives to those who serve him to display his character to people who need his redemption and restoration to his family.

The Text	How God wants those who follow him to demonstrate his character and embrace his mission of restoration
Exodus 22:21–27	
Deuteronomy 10:12–19	
Deuteronomy 24:14–15, 17–22	
Isaiah 42:5–7	

In what ways do these passages expand your understanding of God's passion for redemption and restoration of those who do not know him?

In what ways do these passages expand your vision, compassion, and commitment to the mission of displaying God's character so that all people can know him and experience restoration to his family—the mission to which God has called all who follow him?

3. Caesar Augustus had awarded Philippi status as a Roman colony, so it was home to many Roman citizens who were intensely loyal to the gospel of the Roman Empire. As a community, they were proud of their Roman identity that provided political peace and the most desirable material benefits of the time. However, such benefits came at the price of exemplary loyalty, so city officials were extremely protective of all customs and laws lest "foreigners" undermine their religious and cultural practices and jeopardize the benefits they received from Rome.

In contrast, the gospel of God's kingdom is clear: God's gift of redemption and restoration is available to all people regardless of their social or economic status. No one earns the right to experience God's *shalom* and be restored to the blessings of the *beth ab*. However, redemption is not without cost.

a. What price was paid so that every one of God's lost children could be restored to his family? (See John 3:16; 8:34–36; Romans 5:1–2, 6–11; Galatians 4:4–7.)

b. How does restoration to the *shalom* of God's kingdom differ from how people received peace and prosperity in the kingdom of Rome?

c. How did Paul understand the message of the gospel of Christ in relationship to the mission God gave to his people at Mount Sinai—the mission Jesus fulfilled and extended to all his followers, even to this day? (See Galatians 3:14; Ephesians 2:11–20; Colossians 1:21–23.)

d. What impact does restoration to God's family, God's household, have on those who have been restored and their role in continuing the mission God gave at Mount Sinai? (See Colossians 1:9–14; Titus 2:11–14.)

4. When Paul shared the gospel message in Philippi, who responded, and what is the evidence that she understood the meaning and mission of restoration to God's family and began pursuing it right away? (See Acts 16:13–15.)

Faith Lesson (4 minutes)

From the moment God introduced his plan to redeem his creation from the chaos of sin that came because our ancestors rebelled against him, God chose his human creation to be his partners in that great work (Philippians 1:5–6). Although we are incapable of doing what he has asked—apart from his gracious forgiveness, the power of his presence, the instructions of his inspired Word, and the support of a community—he commands everyone who follows him to be his partner in sharing the gospel message.

God worked his plan of redemption through Abraham and Sarah, choosing their descendants, the people of Israel, to be his priests who would present his love to a broken world. He redeemed them, provided forgiveness through the temple sacrifices, and empowered them to hallow his name (make his reputation known) and thereby bring the light of his redemptive love into the darkness of the nations around them. In gratitude for their redemption, they were to obey him as Lord and extend the reign of his kingdom.

Then God sent the Messiah, Jesus, not only to be the ultimate sacrifice for sin but to show those who followed him how to live as the "household" of God so that the world would see God's love and compassion demonstrated through their daily lives. When the Spirit came on Pentecost, the redeemed community that formed that day was exactly the *beth ab* God intended. They shared all things in common, giving to each according to need, and thousands more were drawn to the Lord through the living example of his human partners.

God chose the apostle Paul to go to the ends of the Roman Empire not simply to proclaim the gospel message but to establish communities of Jesus followers who would continue the redemptive partnership that began with Abraham. They were called to be living examples of what the kingdom of God is like. When Paul went to Philippi, Lydia, a wealthy Gentile merchant, believed and joined the partnership. She opened her home to the new community of people whose citizenship was not in this world but in heaven. By the way they lived, they gave their world a taste of what living in God's kingdom is like.

1. The partnership God began with Abraham continues today. Each of us who is a follower of Jesus is redeemed by his gracious sacrifice, filled with the presence of God's Spirit, and called as a partner in his redemptive community to be a living example of what restoration to God's *shalom* looks like. Have you caught the mission? How do you know?

   What in your life and the way you live needs to better represent your high calling so that others will discover what God is like, submit to his authority as King, and join his household of faith?

2. In Deuteronomy 15:15, God commanded Israel to "remember" (in the sense of recalling and reacting to) God's redemptive work in their lives. Take some time now to read Psalm 103:1–19 and remember, in the way that Moses reminded Israel, what God has done to restore you to his family and to call you as his partner in sharing his gospel of redemption with others. May a better understanding of God's story of redemption inspire us to be less committed to the kingdom of this world and more determined to live like faithful, obedient citizens of God's kingdom so that "he who began a good work in you will carry it on to completion until the day of Christ Jesus."[3]

Closing (1 minute)

Read Matthew 5:14–16 aloud together: "You are the light of the world. A town built on a hill cannot be hidden. Neither do people light a lamp and put it under a bowl. Instead they put it on its stand, and it gives light to everyone in the house. In the same way, let your light shine before others, that they may see your good deeds and glorify your Father in heaven."

Then pray together, thanking God that he is our Father who has gone to great lengths to redeem and restore us to his family. Thank him for trusting us to be his partners in restoring *shalom* to his lost children. May we always be mindful of the great redemptive work God has done for us and throughout history and live every day in response to it. Ask for passion, commitment, and strength from him to be faithful partners who hold his light high in a broken world so that others will come to know and glorify him.

Memorize

You are the light of the world. A town built on a hill cannot be hidden. Neither do people light a lamp and put it under a bowl. Instead they put it on its stand, and it gives light to everyone in the house. In the same way, let your light shine before others, that they may see your good deeds and glorify your Father in heaven.

Matthew 5:14–16

The Gospel of Christ Provokes Imperial Rome

In-Depth Personal Study Sessions

Study One | Paul Shares the Gospel in Philippi

The Very Words of God

As the rain and the snow come down from heaven, and do not return to it without watering the earth and making it bud and flourish, so that it yields seed for the sower and bread for the eater, so is my word that goes out from my mouth: It will not return to me empty, but will accomplish what I desire and achieve the purpose for which I sent it.

Isaiah 55:10–11

Bible Discovery

Seeking Out a Place of Prayer

Throughout history, God's great desire has been for people living in bondage to sin to come to know him through the righteous lives of his human partners as they faithfully display his character. God longs for all people to accept his gift of redemption and be restored to the peace, safety, and blessing of his family. Long before he met Jesus on the road to Damascus, the apostle Paul (whose Jewish name was Saul) was a faithful and righteous Jew fully committed to the mission of being God's partner in fulfilling his plan of redemption.

After Jesus called Paul to witness to Gentiles as well as Jews that God's promise of redemption had come through Jesus' death, resurrection, and ascension, Paul continued the mission. With the same commitment to obey God in all things, he dedicated himself to proclaiming the good news of God's redemption and restoration through Jesus Christ, the Messiah. Paul's faithfulness to the mission that Jesus put before all who follow him exemplifies what it means to "go and make disciples of all nations" (Matthew 28:19).

From one end of the Roman Empire to the other—to Jew and Gentile, rich and poor, male and female, slave and free—Paul shared the good news that Jesus is Savior and Lord. Fulfilling that mission led Paul to the Roman colony of Philippi, one of the most distinctly Roman cities in the empire. Let's see where Paul began teaching and sharing the good news about Jesus when he arrived in a city where the Roman emperor ruled as "lord" and "savior."

1. Paul found great joy in faithfully carrying out the mission God had given to his ancestors. The mission was rooted in the Text that he knew and loved. It fueled his zeal, motivated him to action, and shaped his teaching. In his letter to the Romans who lived in the heart of the empire, the city that was home to Caesar the deified emperor, Paul can barely contain his excitement about the privilege of being God's light to the nations. Read Romans 15:7–13.

   a. What evidence do you see from this passage that Paul considered his obedience to Jesus' call to carry out the "Great Commission" to be an extension of the mission God gave to Israel at Mount Sinai? (See also Deuteronomy 32:43; 2 Samuel 22:50; Psalm 18:49; 117:1; Isaiah 11:10. These are the passages from the Hebrew Text that Paul quotes in this portion of his letter.)

   b. As a Jew and follower of Jesus, how important did Paul think it was to be a light to the Gentiles?

    c. How compelling do you think it would have been to hear the gospel message for the first time from Paul? If you were a Gentile? If you were a Jew?

2. When Paul went into a new community with the gospel message, where did he typically go to teach? (See Acts 13:4–5, 14–16; 14:1.)

    Why was it important for Paul to share the gospel message to the Jewish community first? (See Acts 13:42–49; Romans 1:11–16; 3:1–2.)

    What deep longing in the hearts of the Jewish people likely would have made them interested in, and in many cases receptive to, the gospel message? (See Acts 26:6–7.)

DID YOU KNOW?
A Place of Prayer in Philippi

Luke, the Gentile God-fearer who wrote the book of Acts, was from Philippi. He was with Paul during his visit to that city, so it is likely that he knew about the "place of prayer" Paul went to on the Sabbath. Luke may even have "prayed" with that Jewish community prior to Paul's visit. But what was a place of prayer, and why didn't Paul just go to the synagogue as he so often did?

In Jewish tradition, the word translated *prayer* is the equivalent of *worship*. So, while a follower of Jesus may go to church to *worship*, a Jew goes to synagogue to *pray*. Of course, Jewish worship is not limited to prayer in the sense of talking to God. Jewish "prayer" also includes reciting the *shema* and reading from the Torah and other books in the Tanakh. The place of prayer in Philippi, then, was where Jewish people worshiped God.

The place of prayer likely was an outdoor location rather than a synagogue building, although we cannot know this for sure. The Greek word *proseuche* that is correctly translated "place of prayer" was widely used to describe a synagogue structure and occasionally used to describe a natural outdoor setting used for worship. So it is possible that the place of prayer was outdoors or in a small structure near the river where running water was available for the ritual bathing, or *mikveh*. Although a Jewish burial inscription from the second century AD mentions a synagogue in Philippi, none has ever been found, and it is not known if the one referred to existed when Paul visited the city.[4]

3. What place did Paul seek out to first begin sharing the gospel in Philippi, and where was it located? (See Acts 16:13.)

THINK ABOUT IT
Why Was the Place of Prayer Outside the City?

The Romans were protective of their gods and were concerned about unofficial cults offending the gods, corrupting Roman morals, or introducing un-Roman practices into the community. For this reason, only certain religions were given legal status in the empire. According to the Jewish historian Josephus, Julius Caesar declared Judaism to be an ancient and legal faith.[5] As such, the Jews were allowed to have synagogues in Roman cities. They also were exempt from certain military duties, were permitted to offer sacrifices *for* the emperor rather than *to* him, and were permitted to send the annual temple tax to Jerusalem.

However, anti-Semitism was common in the Roman world, and Jewish communities walked a fine line between acceptance as a legal faith and being judged as a foreign cult. Ancient records provide many examples of Jewish communities appealing to the emperor for relief from discrimination, and imperial decisions usually favored the Jewish minority.[6] But during the reign of Emperor Claudius, 41–54 AD, (who was in power at the time Paul visited Philippi), riots broke out presumably about *Chrestus* (the Latin spelling of *Christ*) and involved the Jewish synagogue community. So, in 41 AD, Claudius expelled the Jews from Rome.[7] This expulsion is the reason Aquila and Priscilla were in Corinth when Paul went to that city (Acts 18:1–2). It may also explain why the place of prayer in Philippi, which was a Roman colony—where life was just as it was in Rome—was outside the city walls.

4. Although we don't know why the Jewish place of prayer, or worship, where Paul first shared the gospel in Philippi was described as being "by the river" (Acts 16:13), there are several possibilities.

    a. On noteworthy occasions, God's people experienced his presence in significant ways near rivers or other bodies of water. In fact, Daniel and Ezekiel, the two great prophets who lived outside the Promised Land, both received their prophetic word by rivers (Ezekiel

1:3; Daniel 10:4–7). And the Mishnah, a later record of Jewish teaching, says, "Outside the land of Israel the Shekinah (the glory presence of God) did not rest upon the prophets except in pure places, by the waters."[8]

What occurred in each of the following passages that would make a riverside location meaningful to Jewish worshipers? (See Genesis 32:22–30; Exodus 14:21–28; Joshua 3:14–17; 2 Kings 2:7–14.)

From the perspective of those who became followers of Jesus, which additional riverside event would be meaningful for those who first heard the gospel message from Paul by the river in Philippi? (See Matthew 3:13–17.)

b. In their efforts to fulfill God's commands for righteous living given at Mount Sinai, the Jewish people developed many traditions for ceremonial cleansing from impurity and sin. For worship in the synagogues of Paul's day, ritual washing (*mikveh*) required fresh, free-flowing water.[9] This could be a reason why the place of prayer was located by the river.

For what kinds of impurity did God require cleansing? (See Leviticus 14:1–9; Psalm 51:1–2; Isaiah 1:15–16.)

A TRIBUTARY OF THE GANGITIS RIVER JUST OUTSIDE THE CITY WALLS OF PHILIPPI WHERE THIS SESSION WAS FILMED.

5. One unusual feature of Luke's account is that he mentions women participating in the Sabbath gathering, but no men. Men would be expected at such a gathering, and at one point in Jewish tradition—possibly even during this time period—ten men needed to be present in order to have formal prayer (remember, prayer is worship) as a community. Nevertheless, these women had gathered for worship, so what did Paul do as was his custom? (See Acts 16:13.)

Although we don't know whether Paul's teaching focused on the synagogue reading for the day or another subject, what do we learn about what he taught and its impact on his listeners? (See Acts 16:14–15.)

Paul is sometimes accused of having a low view of women, but it is apparent from his visit to Philippi that he initiated contact with women as well as Gentiles in order to share the gospel message. In his letters of encouragement to Jesus followers in Philippi and Rome, who does Paul clearly include as being partners in the gospel with him? (See Romans 16:12–16; Philippians 1:4–6.)

DID YOU KNOW?
God Prepared the Way

During the first century, Gentiles, especially women, were drawn to the Jewish faith communities where they were introduced to the God of the Hebrews and learned the teachings of the Torah. So before Paul even reached the Roman colony of Philippi, there was a community of people that included Gentiles and women who worshiped the Lord! Although the community appears to have been small, there is no doubt that God had been at work preparing the soil for the seed of the good news that Paul and others would sow. When Paul arrived to extend God's partnership in the gospel to anyone who wanted to be a part of it—Gentile or Jew, male or female, slave or free—his faithfulness bore fruit.

Reflection

Beginning at Mount Sinai, God called his people to be his priests, to bring the message of redemption—the good news that he is Savior and Lord—to a broken world. Israel's mission was to present the gospel message by their words and by their life example. Jesus came to continue that mission through his teaching and example and fulfill it through his death, resurrection, and ascension. Before he ascended to his throne in heaven, Jesus commissioned his disciples to go into all the world and continue the mission. That same mission, given to God's people so long ago, is the mission Jesus gave to Saul, who we now know as Paul, which led him to Philippi.

From the beginning, God has prepared the way for the gospel message and has anointed it as it is lived and spoken by his faithful followers. We see that preparation clearly in Paul's visit to Philippi, where God had prepared a place of prayer. Even though it was a Roman colony and few people there—if any—had ever heard of Jesus, there was a place where Paul could safely present the gospel. There were people—just a few apparently—who already knew and put their faith in the Lord and worshiped him on the Sabbath.

As God's partners in his great work of redemption, we now share the same responsibility as Paul. God calls us not only to bring the message but to be the message. We may question our ability to accomplish the work or doubt that it will make any difference in the broken culture in which we live, but God who redeemed us has given us our mission and has prepared the way for us. We are responsible to live out our faith so that others may know him and we can, as Paul did, count on the promise of Isaiah 55:10–11:

> *As the rain and the snow come down from heaven, and do not return to it without watering the earth and making it bud and flourish, so that it yields seed for the sower and bread for the eater, so is my word that goes out from my mouth: It will not return to me empty, but will accomplish what I desire and achieve the purpose for which I sent it.*

As each of us goes to our "Philippi," the place and circumstance to which God leads us, he will have gone before us. We can be confident that our task will accomplish the purpose God intends.

Before Paul went to Philippi, he already had shared the gospel in some prominent cities. Why do you think he considered it worthwhile to spend several days with such a seemingly small group of Jews and Gentile God-fearers?

Why is it important for us, as followers of Jesus today, to keep proclaiming the gospel of Jesus even when it seems as if few people are interested in what God has given us to say?

To what extent have you underestimated how God can use you—regardless of your past mistakes, struggles, or "qualifications"—in the lives of people who need redemption and restoration to God's family?

What steps will you take, starting now, to be more attentive to God's leading and more obedient to his calling?

Study Two | Paul's Message Finds an Open Heart

The Very Words of God

In all my prayers for all of you, I always pray with joy because of your partnership in the gospel from the first day until now, being confident of this, that he who began a good work in you will carry it on to completion until the day of Christ Jesus.

Philippians 1:4–6

Bible Discovery

God's People Gather and God's Kingdom Comes!

Luke's account of Paul's ministry in Philippi gives us a compelling picture of God's love for all his children who are outside the protection and care of his family, his *beth ab*. It shows his faithfulness in seeking and redeeming them so that they too can become his partners in redemption, his instruments of grace and love in the world. What are the chances that a Gentile woman from Thyatira and a Jewish rabbi (who had tried to take his message elsewhere) would meet in a small worship gathering on the outskirts of Philippi? What are the chances that their interaction would lead to a community of believers being established in a Roman colony? What are the chances that that fledgling community would demonstrate to those of us who follow Jesus nearly two thousand years later how to live as God's partners in redemption in our world?

Clearly God is at work leading his people, preparing hearts, and drawing sinners to redemption so that his kingdom comes!

When Paul sat down among the women gathered outside Philippi for prayer on the Sabbath, he assumed the role of a Jewish teacher and demonstrated from the Hebrew Text the truth that Jesus is Messiah. Paul was uniquely qualified to teach the gospel as he did. He had spent his early childhood in Tarsus in Cilicia, a commercial hub known for its great wealth and a university equal to those in Athens or Alexandria. As the son of a faithful Jewish family, it is likely Paul received an excellent early education in the Greek and Roman worldviews as well as in the Torah.

Later, Paul lived in Jerusalem where he studied under Gamaliel, one of the most highly respected Torah experts and the greatest of all Jewish sages. To be a student of Gamaliel, Paul must have been brilliant (and inspired) in his knowledge and interpretation of the Hebrew Text. Gamaliel, whose interpretations of the Text were often similar to those of Jesus, clearly influenced Paul's teaching. In addition, he taught Greek Wisdom so that his disciples could apply the Torah to the Hellenistic worldview of Imperial Rome. Like Moses, Paul had an unusual background of training and experience that prepared him for exactly the task God intended. As they were growing up, Moses and Paul could not have known how God would use them in his plan, yet each was prepared for his task in every way.[10]

Lydia, the other key player in Luke's account (Acts 16:13–15), entered the scene prepared to respond to the gospel message. She was what is known as a God-fearer, one of a significant number of Gentiles in the Roman Empire who had joined the Jewish community in worshiping God. These men and women renounced allegiance to their pagan gods and the practices associated with their worship and chose to worship the God of the Jews. They lived by the moral law of the Torah, although they usually did not become "fully" Jewish in terms of eating a kosher diet, wearing tassels, being circumcised, or following the laws of ritual purity.

We don't know what attracted Lydia to the God of the Jews, but we do know that she had been drawn toward God and worshiped him with the Jewish people. So it appears the Jewish community, small as it was, was being a kingdom of priests in their world just as God intended. Let's consider how Lydia responded when Paul came with the teaching that Jesus was the Messiah promised in Scripture.

1. Paul taught the gospel message wherever he went. Read Acts 16:14; 17:1–4, 10–12, 16–20, 33–34, taking note of the words used to describe the people who heard and believed Paul's message. What do you learn about them, particularly those who were not Jews?

Why is it significant that in the very class- and gender-conscious Roman world, many Gentiles—even some of notable social, economic, or political status—would associate themselves with the Jewish people and their God?

DATA FILE
Who Are the God-Fearers?
Many accounts of Paul teaching the gospel in the book of Acts mention people known as God-fearers, God-fearing Gentiles, or God-fearing Greeks. These were Gentiles who were attracted to the Jewish God and participated in synagogue worship and the life of their local Jewish community. Although there was disagreement within the Jewish (and, later, the early Christian) community as to how much of the Torah God-fearing Gentiles should be required to observe—whether or not they must fully convert and practice circumcision, wear tassels, obey purity rituals, and follow a kosher diet—there is no doubt that they were active participants in the community of God's people. They knew the Hebrew Bible, had renounced their pagan gods and sinful lifestyle, and became a natural gateway for the gospel into the Gentile world.

Several inscriptions referring to God-fearers among the Jewish community have been found in the ruins of Miletus and Sardis, but the clearest evidence of their association is found on a marble pillar in Aphrodisias. Called a *stele*, the pillar has legible inscriptions (in Greek) on two of its four faces.[11] It is believed the pillar dates from the time when the early church was growing in Aphrodisias. Scholars are also quite certain that the pillar is associated with a synagogue or a charitable undertaking, most likely a soup kitchen or food pantry, of the synagogue community.

(LEFT) *STELE* **WITH LISTS OF NAMES OF PARTICIPANTS IN THE SYNAGOGUE'S CHARITABLE UNDERTAKING. (RIGHT)** *OSOI THEOSEBIS.*

The lists on the pillar are intriguing. One face (left side, left photo) lists individuals who contributed to the construction of a new building. The other face (right side, left photo) has two lists of people associated with the project. The first group of fifty-five names (some Greek, others Hebrew) are under the heading "Jews." This list also designates three proselytes or converts, meaning three Gentiles who had fully converted to Judaism (including circumcision). The second group (right photo) is under the heading *theosebes*, which means God-fearers. These apparently were Gentiles who had been attracted to God by the faithful living of the Jewish community and, although they had not completely converted to Judaism, had abandoned their pagan gods and practices and identified with the Jewish community and their God.

The *stele* is significant because it provides archeological evidence of communities that are described in both the New Testament and Jewish sources. Even before the Christian message came to the Roman world, God had been drawing pagan Gentiles to himself! Wherever the early followers of Jesus went, they found people of the Text who eagerly accepted the good news that Jesus, the long-awaited Messiah, had come.

To see the pillar at Aphrodisias with its list of God-fearers is to see passionate devotion to God in action. How could any of these witnesses have imagined that their faith in God would speak to their world and still speak so powerfully today? We can find great encouragement in the fact that if we live faithfully and speak clearly of our love for Jesus, God has and is always preparing an audience that is eager to hear the good news.

2. Lydia is singled out as a person who opened her heart to Paul's message when he spoke in Philippi. What does the Text reveal about her, her occupation, and who she was spiritually? (See Acts 16:14.)

PERSONAL PROFILE
Who Was Lydia?

We know from the account of Paul's visit to Philippi in Acts that Lydia was a merchant of purple cloth and came from the city of Thyatira. But those facts don't mean much to us unless we dig a bit deeper.

Lydia was known by her personal name rather than by her family or husband's name, which would have been unusual for a Roman woman. So Lydia was likely of Greek heritage, not Roman. A woman of accomplishment and influence, she had her own household and had achieved significant status, wealth, and social importance in the class-bound Roman culture.[12]

How did she achieve such status? She was involved in the trade of a luxury item known as purple cloth, which was created using an extremely expensive purple dye (*porphyria*, in Greek) made from the murex shellfish. The dye was produced on the eastern coast of the Mediterranean Sea, including Israel and Phoenicia (derived from the Greek word meaning "land of the purple"). Ancient sources record that it took 10,000 murex snails to make one gram of dye, so few could afford the luxury of a purple garment.

Historically, Jewish people were known for the production of the purple dye. It was the color God specified for the curtains and veil in the tabernacle and temple. It was also used in the ephod the priests wore when they served in those places. And, it was the color of the single blue/purple thread God commanded his people to place in the tassels they wore to remind them that they were his holy kingdom of priests called to display him to the nations. As a merchant of purple, Lydia may have come to know the God of the Jews through her involvement in a trade that was significantly Jewish.

By the first century, the color purple had become significant in the Roman Empire. The color purple designated the empire's upper class, so there was an imperial monopoly of it. As a merchant of purple cloth, Lydia may have manufactured the dye, dyed and sold the cloth, or both. Because trade in "purple" was monopolized by Roman authorities, Lydia would have had extensive connections with the imperial government (called "Caesar's household") and thus would have been an influential person in the Roman colony of Philippi.

It is amazing to realize that the first recorded person to respond to the good news in Philippi was an influential Gentile woman who had the means to provide a place where the "Jesus community" could meet. Think of God's preparation for the gospel message in Philippi!

3. After the Lord opened Lydia's heart to the gospel and she was baptized, what did she immediately do for Paul and his companions who had recently arrived in Philippi? (See Acts 16:15.)

In what ways did Lydia's response differ from the typical Roman view of how things were done, especially for a woman who had social standing and financial means?

What do you suppose might have influenced or led Lydia to begin using her resources to advance the kingdom of heaven?

How might her actions have influenced and encouraged other new believers in Philippi?

4. God has chosen human partners—both male and female, Jew and Gentile—to make known his message of redemption. During Old Testament times, life in the Middle East revolved around the family patriarch. Most often men—Moses, David, Elijah, Hezekiah, and Ezra, to name a few—played the leading roles in God's redemptive story. Yet God's mission is for *all* of his people. At certain moments in history, contrary to established cultural practices, he advances his work of redemption in unexpected ways. God chooses the youngest over the firstborn. He uses a Gentile rather than a Jew. He sends an infant rather than a war hero. He makes himself known through a woman rather than a man.

The genealogy of Jesus, God's chosen Redeemer, a descendant of Abraham and Sarah through the line of David (Matthew 1:1–16) is an example of God doing the unexpected. It includes mention of women who typically were not included in genealogies and Gentile women, which is doubly significant.[13] What do you learn about the following four women who God brought into his story as partners in his plan of redemption that makes their participation unexpected, and what impact does their experience in God's plan have on you?

a. Rahab (see Matthew 1:5; Joshua 2; 6:25)

b. Ruth (see Matthew 1:5; Ruth 1–4; Deuteronomy 23:3–6[14])

c. Bathsheba—Uriah's wife, later David's wife (see Matthew 1:6; 2 Samuel 11; 12:24–25)

d. Mary (see Matthew 1:16, 18–25; Luke 1:26–56)

5. God's preparation for and advancement of the gospel in the Roman Empire frequently involved women, and often Gentile women. This was a radical message in a culture where status and class determined a person's value and destiny—even whether they were allowed to wear clothing of the color purple! As you read the following passages describing God's redemptive community in the Roman Empire, what are some of the ways women served as God's partners in the mission and in the growing community of Jesus followers? (See Acts 1:12–16; 2:17–18, 21; 5:14–16; 18:1–3, 18–19, 24–28; Romans 16:1–15; Philemon 1–2.)

Reflection

I am humbled and blessed as I consider how God prepared the
way for Paul to share the gospel and for it to make an impact in
Philippi. Long before Paul approached the city and shared God's
message, Lydia was there. As Paul was obedient to God's leading,
God opened Lydia's heart and began a work that advanced the
kingdom of God in her world and continues to advance God's
kingdom today. I believe there are two lessons to be gained from
Lydia's story.

First, as we choose to follow God and be the gospel in flesh
wherever God leads us, we can be sure that he has gone before
us and will have the right people in place to anoint what we
do in his service. If we live as God's word in flesh—not simply
bringing God's message but *being* God's message—people will
respond and our lives, empowered by God, will bear fruit.

I continue to be amazed by how this very project—the That the
World May Know study series—demonstrates the truth of how
God works. I followed God's leading to study the Bible in context and teach it in a Christian school and in local churches.
Through circumstances completely in God's control, he brought
me into contact with Ed and Elsa Prince and, through them, with
Focus on the Family. The result is that my teaching, which I was
doing already, has become part of a twenty-five-year project that
continues even as I write these words. I trust that the path God
has prepared and the mission he has given to me will produce
much fruit for his kingdom.

Who has God used to prepare the way for you to understand
and respond to the gospel message of Jesus?

What about that person and his or her message stood out to you and displayed God in such a way that you chose to respond and join God's family as a follower of Jesus?

How do you see God preparing the way and leading you to be his message in your world and bear fruit for his kingdom?

Second, there is a sense in which each of us is a "Lydia." Lydia was a merchant who worshiped the God of Israel, and that did not change when she met Paul and became a follower of Jesus. If we follow Jesus, our life circumstances are arranged by God to provide us opportunities to put him on display and be his message to others. Just as Lydia served God by being a dye merchant, God leads us to our circumstances in life: the college we attend, the place we live, the career we pursue, the hobbies we have, the family and friends whose lives we share. In all these things we can serve God as his priests who put him on display in everything we say and do.

God uses ordinary people in normal life situations to be messengers who proclaim his good news—just as he used Lydia. In what specific ways are you a living display of the good news of God's kingdom to any of the following: your classmates, those who live in your community, your fellow workers, those you get to know through your hobbies, your close friends and family?

Study Three | A Colony of Heaven in a Broken World

The Very Words of God

> *Whatever happens, conduct yourselves in a manner worthy of the gospel of Christ. Then, whether I come and see you or only hear about you in my absence, I will know that you stand firm in the one Spirit, striving together as one for the faith of the gospel.*
>
> *Philippians 1:27*

Bible Discovery

Be the Message: Live Like God Has Come to Town!

Philippi was a Roman colony,[15] designated as such so that its citizens would enjoy all the benefits of living in Rome and serve as an exemplary model of Roman culture and influence in Macedonia. Roman colonies were established, in a sense, to be a beachhead for extending the culture and control of Rome into a larger area. A colony was a kind of advertising campaign that demonstrated what it meant to be Roman, a loyal and privileged subject of divine Caesar.

It is likely that most of the people living in Philippi were Roman citizens and former soldiers who were intensely loyal to the Roman Empire and to Rome, the mother city. They were obsessed with living as if they were in Rome. They honored the gods of Rome and worshiped the emperor. They upheld the laws and protected the customs of Rome. They experienced the pleasures and safety that Rome provided. Their primary identity was to proclaim with pride, "I am Roman."

But Philippi was home to another colony, a colony of citizens of heaven. These citizens believed Paul's message, the good news that Jesus—Messiah, Son of God, anointed King, and Savior of the world—had come to restore them to God's kingdom. They professed their loyalty to Jesus and were dedicated to extending the reign of his kingdom on earth. How influential a beachhead would the Jesus followers establish in their community? What impact would the colony of heaven have on Philippi?

1. The followers of Jesus in Philippi chose loyalty to a kingdom and a king greater than that of Rome and its emperor. Which metaphor did Paul use to identify those who followed Jesus in Philippi, and why would this have been a meaningful expression of their status? (See Philippians 3:20–21.)

   Because of their identity as citizens of heaven, how did Paul instruct the Philippians to conduct themselves? (See Philippians 1:27.)

   What dangers would Jesus followers in Philippi face because of their choice to live as citizens of heaven—in a sense becoming foreigners in their own city? (See Philippians 1:29–30.)

DID YOU KNOW?

The word translated *citizenship* in Philippians 3:20 is *politeuma*, which means "to live or act as a citizen." Paul wanted the followers of Jesus in Philippi to understand that they were no longer primarily citizens of Philippi or even Rome: above all else, they were citizens of heaven.[13] They were to heaven what Philippi was to Rome.

Just as a Roman citizen in Philippi would seek to behave as a citizen worthy of the good news of divine Caesar, Paul commands the citizens of heaven to be worthy of the good news of Jesus Christ (Philippians 1:27). They were to focus their lives not on earthly things (the values of the kingdoms of this world) but according to the laws and customs of heaven itself. This is how God's kingdom comes on earth as it is in heaven.

2. God's great story of redemption is replete with examples of how he seeks out his children who are separated from him, restores those who believe his message to the "Father's house," and invites them to join the story by becoming instruments of his love to a broken world. Often the evidence that a person's newfound faith is genuine can be seen when that person joins the mission God gave to his people at Mount Sinai and lives to display God's character, honor, and reputation, and thereby extend God's reign in the world. What impact did the gospel message, as presented by Paul, have on Lydia and in what three ways did she respond? (See Acts 16:13–15.)

What did Lydia do as a sign that she and her household would be loyal followers of Jesus, had joined the family of God, and would live to extend the kingdom of heaven? (See Acts 16:15; also Romans 6:4; Galatians 3:26–29; Colossians 2:9–12.)

FOR GREATER UNDERSTANDING
The Baptism of Households

Luke's account of Lydia's conversion mentions that she and her whole household were baptized. While it may seem unusual to us, the practice of household baptism is mentioned in accounts of other Gentiles who declared their commitment to Jesus and joined the family of God. This subject has engendered much discussion regarding the nature of such conversions and baptisms, but that is not our focus in this study.

Given the limitations of our study, it is important to note two things. First, entire households believed and joined the community of Jesus. Second, the inclusion of an entire household in baptism did not necessarily imply a faith commitment by every member of that household.

In Roman culture, the household—or likely the head of the household—determined the religious practices of the entire household, including its slaves.[17] When Lydia believed and her household was baptized, they made a public declaration that the Lord alone, the God of the Jews, was their God. We can think of the baptism of Lydia's household as a declaration similar to what Ruth declared to Naomi, her Jewish mother-in-law: "Your people will be my people and your God my God" (Ruth 1:16).

God's intention in spreading the gospel message to every corner of the world was not simply to acquire new converts but to build communities of believers who encouraged and strengthened one another in demonstrating to their culture what it looks like when God is in charge. His intent is for his people to display his *shalom*—to display his kingdom on earth as it is in heaven. What did Lydia provide for Paul and the community of believers in Philippi, and how important was this service to the growth of God's kingdom there? (See Acts 16:15, 40.)

3. As is true for all who follow Jesus, Lydia and the other new believers in Philippi had a mission to fulfill. They were to be God's witnesses (Isaiah 43:10) and establish a beachhead for God's kingdom in their city. In the biblical world, a kingdom was any place or situation where the king was obeyed. So to be a colony of God's kingdom, they would have to *be* God's message through their obedience to his commands, his way of living. How could they accomplish this? (See 2 Corinthians 3:18.)

From a practical standpoint, God's people become his witnesses as we let him take charge and display his *shalom*—his merciful, redemptive love—through our interactions with others. Consider what the Bible says about God's characteristic love and mercy, and write down ways you can be a bearer of his image as you live each moment of life.

The Text	How I can be a bearer of God's image
Compassion: Deuteronomy 15:12–15; 24:14–15; Matthew 25:24–40; Ephesians 4:32	
Care for foreigners, widows, orphans: Exodus 22:21–22; Leviticus 19:33–34; Deuteronomy 10:17–19; 14:28–29; 24:19–22	
Meeting the needs of the poor: Leviticus 19:9–10; 23:22; 25:35–38; Deuteronomy 15:7–11; Proverbs 19:17	
Justice for oppressed: Deuteronomy 1:16-17; 23:15–16; 27:19; Proverbs 22:22–23	
Love for one's enemies: Proverbs 25:21	
Practice hospitality: 1 Peter 4:8–11	
Bear God's image: Matthew 5:14–16, 43–48; 1 Peter 2:12	

4. In light of God's calling for his redeemed people to live in unity and display his character in every word and action, why was it important for Euodia and Syntyche to reconcile their differences, and what might be the consequences if they did not? (See Philippians 1:3–6, 27; 4:1–9; John 17:20–23.)

THE THEATER OF PHILIPPI WHERE THE ROMANS CONDUCTED GLADIATORIAL CONTESTS

REFLECTION

On Pentecost, God planted a colony of heaven on earth, and thousands were drawn to the Messiah. As he traveled and taught, Paul planted colonies of God's kingdom in Antioch of Pisidia, Iconium, Lystra, Derbe, and Philippi. Each served as a beachhead where God's kingdom extended its reign, as people believed and obeyed his will. People who did not know God were drawn toward heaven not simply because someone told them about God but because they experienced a taste of what heaven was like—because citizens of heaven lived in their town!

The community of Jesus followers in Philippi met together in Lydia's house. That small colony of heaven became known for acts of *shalom* to those in need. It began to multiply. Its members joined in partnership with the gospel and supported Paul's ministry through words, prayer, and generous financial help (Philippians 1:5). They became the "word in flesh"—a living expression of God's love that made a powerful impact in a broken world.

It is difficult for me to write this, but we must ask the question. Does the community of faith today have the reputation of being a colony of heaven where people see what life is like when God comes to town? I am afraid, to a large extent, that the Christian community—from small local churches to denominations to particular viewpoints within the faith—is defined more by our disagreement, dislike, mistrust, criticism, and condemnation than as a team of "gladiators" who battle the Evil One and his influence. We so often turn on each other, in words, attitudes, and sometimes even violence.

How often have we compromised the validity of God's redemption with our disunity and discord? Why should a disbelieving world listen to our claim to demonstrate what heaven is like when we fight against each other while the Evil One attacks us and tears us apart like a lion? We cannot be a colony, citizens of heaven, living proof of what heaven will be like if we fight one another. Paul knew that and strongly instructed the Philippians to change their ways. Was anyone listening? Euodia and Syntyche? Is anyone listening today?

> What is your commitment to live each day as a citizen of heaven, as one who has been redeemed and restored to God's family by his powerful love?

> What do you think it looks like to be a citizen of heaven in your community among your family, friends, and neighbors?

How might a colony of heaven distinguish itself and be a
light of God's love where you live?

THE POWERS OF DARKNESS

Paul walked into Philippi in 50 AD, proclaiming the good news that Jesus, God's Messiah, the Savior of the world had come and opened the doors of the kingdom of heaven to everyone who believed in him. Many believed and submitted to God's reign in their lives. Living in Philippi as citizens of heaven, they became a faithful, vibrant community that extended God's kingdom one person, one household at a time.

However, another kingdom already existed in Philippi. The city was a Roman colony, literally an extension of the kingdom of Imperial Rome. It too proclaimed a gospel: the official good news that Caesar, *divi filius* (the son of god), the savior of the world, was lord of all. Although Paul never attacked or criticized Caesar's gospel, his proclamation of the gospel of God's kingdom raised serious questions about the validity of Caesar's kingdom.

Like Jesus before him, Paul understood that he was involved in a great clash of kingdoms. Paul understood that the enemy of God's kingdom was not any person who tried to silence him or any nation that opposed him. The enemy was not the corrupt Jewish leadership or the Roman authorities. The real enemy was far greater than Rome could ever be: it was Satan, the Evil One, who from the beginning of God's story rose up against the Almighty.

Ejected from heaven, Satan is the source of evil behind all human wickedness and injustice. He captures the minds and hearts of people and uses them to further his kingdom, the kingdom of this world, which thrives on the chaos that results from defying

God. He does not easily surrender the territory he has captured. So it should not surprise us that a fierce struggle broke out when Paul began proclaiming in Philippi that the kingdom of God had come.

The first sign of that struggle came from an unlikely source. A young girl, a slave to the power of the Evil One and her owners, began a protest that threatened to interrupt Paul's proclamation of the gospel of Jesus Christ. Although the power of evil is very great, the kingdom of God is greater—and it prevails. So in the name of Jesus, the King of kings, Paul confronted "the powers of this dark world" (Ephesians 6:12) and set the young girl free.

Though the story of this unnamed girl takes up only three verses in the Bible, it is a powerful plea for each person who has been restored to God's family and is called to represent his kingdom on earth to reach out and offer hope and help to those who live in chaos. Her gripping story reminds us that the grasp of the Evil One is powerless when confronted by the power of the Lord Jesus. It helps us to recognize that the enemy of God's kingdom is not those who disagree with us, those who believe differently than we do, or those who oppose us. The enemy is the very one Jesus and Paul overcame, and by the name of Jesus we have the power to overcome him as well.

Opening Thoughts (3 minutes)

The Very Words of God

> Live as free people, but do not use your freedom as a cover-up for evil;
> live as God's slaves.

1 Peter 2:16

Think About It

Throughout history people have valued their freedom—their ability to live life as they desire, to raise their families, to engage in productive and profitable work, and to participate in mutually beneficial community relationships. When one person, group, or nation exerts power over another, it results in a loss of freedom—perhaps a limitation as to where one may live, how one may earn a living, or who one may associate with. Of course, the total loss of freedom, slavery, may lead to great personal suffering, physical harm, or even death.

How often do we give thoughtful consideration to the freedom we have in Christ?

How highly do we value, respect, use, and guard that freedom?

What is at risk if we use our freedom carelessly or are unaware of the ways by which we become enslaved to the kingdom of this world?

Video Notes (30 minutes)

The kingdom of God confronts the powers of darkness

A young slave girl

Slavery in the Roman Empire

A python spirit

The Oracle at Delphi

Hungry for a word from the gods

Rock of Gaia and the Pythia

Receiving an oracle from Apollo

The last oracle

Set free . . .

From bondage at the temple of Apollo

By the power of Jesus' name

Bought with a price to serve Jesus

Video Discussion (6 minutes)

1. What new insights into everyday life in the Roman
    Empire did you gain by learning more about the practice
    of slavery during the time of Jesus and the apostles?

    How does that knowledge help you to understand why
    the gospel message was often viewed as "radical" or "dan-
    gerous" and caused such concern for those in power?

2. It is obvious from what remains of the structures at Del-
    phi that the oracle and temple of Apollo were extremely
    important to people. Locate Delphi on the map and con-
    sider the effort people expended to get there. Even today
    access roads through this mountainous region are wind-
    ing, steep, and narrow.

    What do the size and
    remote location of Del-
    phi say to you about
    the hunger of ancient
    people to receive
    divine counsel from
    their gods?

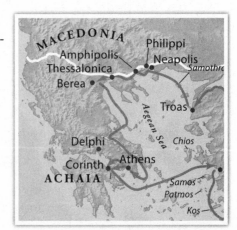

THE APOLLO TEMPLE AT DELPHI HIGH ON THE SLOPE OF MOUNT PARNASSUS

In what ways do you think people today seek to satisfy their yearning for supernatural counsel and power, and how much effort do they put into that pursuit?

3. What new understanding did you gain about the power of the kingdom of this world to hold people in bondage and to oppose the gospel message and the advancement of the kingdom of heaven?

4. Imagine yourself as a person who lived in the "slave society" of the Roman Empire during the first century. How might your knowledge of slavery and the process of manumission (or other means by which a slave could be freed by his or her owner) impact your understanding of the gospel message and your response to it?

Small Group Bible Discovery and Discussion (15 minutes)

Free, Yet a Slave of God

Slavery was a significant part of life in the Roman Empire during New Testament times.[1] The empire had become a "slave society" built and maintained by hundreds of thousands of slaves. There were no trades or social structures that were not dependent on slave labor. Even most gladiators were slaves. Some estimates indicate that one in four or as many as one in three of the Roman Empire's 70 million people were slaves![2] In the larger cities such as Rome or Ephesus and in Roman colonies such as Philippi, slaves would have accounted for an even higher portion of the population.

The gulf between slave and free was enormous. Socially, slaves were considered part of the owner's household or family. But by law, slaves were property—just above livestock. When a person became a slave, all status, security, and stability vanished. Contracts the person may have had or debts owed to the person were no longer valid. Political positions were voided. Marriages were terminated. If a slave gave testimony in court, torture was used to prove that the slave was telling the truth.

Any free citizen could own a slave, so most Romans owned one or more, and the very wealthy may have owned hundreds. Typically, a person who had been sold and became a slave remained a slave for life. There were few ways out of that bondage. Some slaves obtained freedom from their owners as the reward for their faithful service; some were released so that they might marry their owners; and some were manumitted. In other cases, a family might remain enslaved for generations.

Although readers of the New Testament today may not readily understand the images and metaphors of slavery that Paul and other writers used to communicate the gospel message, these images communicated vividly to people who lived during the first century. Let's consider how Paul used the process of sacred manumission as a metaphor for what Jesus did to set the human race free from bondage to sin, and why those who follow him are both "free" and "slaves."

1. What essential truth did Paul communicate in the following passages that would have shocked his listeners, especially those who were Roman citizens, not slaves? (See Romans 6:16–21; 7:21–24; 8:1–2; Galatians 4:8; Titus 3:3.)

    What impact do you think this message may have had on Paul's hearers?

What hope do people have for escaping this condition on their own?

DATA FILE
The Practice of Sacred Manumission

Many worship cults in the ancient world offered sacred manumission as a way for slaves to be set free from their owners. The process followed a generally accepted pattern[3] that required the slave to save a sum of money equal to his or her worth. Although few slaves could accumulate enough money to pay their own ransom, those who did would entrust the money to the temple priests (or priestesses) for safekeeping. Next, the slave would have to persuade the owner to sell the slave to the temple. If the owner was agreeable, the owner and slave would go to the temple where, before witnesses, the owner sold the slave to the god for the amount entrusted to

POLYGONAL MASONRY WALL AT THE APOLLO TEMPLE IN DELPHI

the temple priests. The owner went away with the money, and the slave was then considered redeemed—a free person.

Even then, the person wasn't entirely free. He or she now belonged to the god. Out of gratitude, manumitted slaves were often devoted to the service, worship, and praise of the god who had set them free.

Much of our knowledge about sacred manumission comes from the Apollo temple at Delphi, including the polygonal masonry wall that serves as a retaining wall for the temple platform. This unusual structure is enormous—nearly 12 feet tall and 100 yards long—and can't be avoided as a person approaches the Apollo temple. An example of highly skilled masonry work, the wall is made of randomly shaped polygonal stone blocks—some as large as six feet across—that fit together perfectly without mortar. The exposed faces of the stones are finished smooth to allow for carved inscriptions.

Each inscription—and there are more than 1,200 of them—records the manumission of a slave by the god Apollo at his temple in Delphi. Stone after stone expresses gratitude and admiration for the god who set slaves free. It is deeply moving to stand in front of the wall and imagine the suffering of the slaves who went there to find freedom, and the exhilaration they experienced when they were set free.

2. Paul's explanation of how deliverance from slavery to sin occurs in God's kingdom sounds similar to the practice of manumission. But there is a key difference. Slaves in the Roman Empire had to raise their own purchase price. Who pays the price of redemption from slavery to sin in the kingdom of heaven? (See Romans 3:23–24; 8:3; 1 Corinthians 6:19–20; Ephesians 1:3, 7–8; 1 Timothy 2:3–6.)

"Bought with a price" is the very phrase used to describe a slave who was manumitted by a temple. What might people have thought and how might they have responded when they learned that God himself paid the price to set people free from slavery to sin?

3. A slave freed by sacred manumission was no longer bound to whatever had made him or her a slave, but instead became a slave to the god who arranged the redemption. The manumitted slave was committed to a new purpose in life: to serve the god by honoring, worshiping, and proclaiming the god's greatness in everything he or she did. Let's consider the freedom that the blood of Jesus has bought for those who accept God's gift of redemption from slavery to sin.

    a. A manumitted slave was said to be "redeemed," and Paul occasionally used the same term to describe God's gift of grace through Jesus that sets those who believe free from bondage to sin. But for those who were familiar with the Hebrew Text, the word had a greater meaning than manumission alone. In ancient times, a patriarch would rescue or redeem a marginalized family member, paying whatever debt kept that person in bondage, in order to restore the person to the community and to the protection of the family household (*beth ab*). What does God's work to redeem us from bondage to sin and death also provide that we could never receive through any other means? (See Galatians 4:4–7; Ephesians 1:3–8; Colossians 1:13–14.)

b.　Paul eagerly declared that those who have been bought by the blood of Jesus are free—free from sin, death, and everything else that controls and keeps people in bondage. What freedom does the blood of Jesus buy for those who follow him, and what responsibility comes with that freedom? (See Romans 6:6–7, 17–23; Galatians 5:1; 1 Peter 2:16; Revelation 1:5–6.)

c.　As you read the following passages—Romans 1:1; 1 Corinthians 4:1; 2 Corinthians 6:4; Philippians 1:1; Titus 1:1—notice how Paul described the nature of his relationship with God and how seriously he viewed his role as a *doulos* (meaning "slave" or "servant"). In what ways does his understanding of being a follower of Jesus and serving God as a *slave* challenge our thinking about what it means to follow Jesus, to say we belong to him, and to serve him?

Faith Lesson (5 minutes)

It can be difficult for Western people who love the ideas of freedom, independence, and democracy to think of being a slave to anyone, even to God. We much prefer the idea of being a *servant* to that of being a *slave*. But the Scripture is clear. If we have been redeemed by the blood of Jesus, we belong to God. We are free to be his slaves.

The Greek word *doulos,* which can mean "slave" or "servant," is often translated as "servant" in English Bibles. That usage is more a function of the cultural situation when the first English Bibles were translated than how the word was understood during the first century. In a culture where slaves accounted for nearly a third of the population, few people had servants, and they would have understood that Paul intended "slave" to be his meaning. So how did we come to understand our role as "servants" of God rather than his "slaves"? John MacArthur points out that early English Bible translations were affected by the controversial slave trade in the British Empire. Using the term "slaves of Christ" seemed too negative, so translators chose "servant" instead.[4]

We must be careful not to minimize what God has done for us. He has redeemed us—just as certainly as he redeemed the Hebrews from the brutal bondage of slavery to Pharaoh—from bondage to the Evil One that inevitably leads to death. Through the shed blood of Jesus, God has set us free to receive eternal life! It is our incredible privilege and honor to belong to him and with hearts of gratitude become his "slaves," laboring for the advancement of his kingdom.

So, who really owns us? Will we choose to be slaves of Jesus, not just servants?[5]

1. The Heidelberg Catechism, which I learned as a child, reads, "My only comfort in life and in death is that I am not my own but belong, body and soul, to my faithful Savior Jesus Christ." In Jesus, we belong to God; he owns us. We are not servants who are free to leave his service to serve another. What does it mean to you to be a "slave" owned by God?

2. A servant may choose how to serve his or her employer; a slave must obey the owner's command. Jesus commands those who follow him to submit completely to his will and to walk as he walks. Are you willing to be God's slave and serve him according to all that he commands?

3. As people redeemed by God, we are set free from the power of all other bondage: to self, to Satan, to sensual pleasure and lust, to material accumulation, and to accomplishment. As free people, we must live in total submission to the One to whom we belong. Are you so completely owned by God that you will not become enslaved to evil again?

4. When we view ourselves as slaves to Christ—owned by him, accountable to serve him completely—how does it affect the way we express honor to him, worship him, proclaim his greatness, and display his character to the world around us?

Closing (1 minute)

Read 1 Corinthians 6:19–20 aloud together: "Do you not know that . . . you are not your own; you were bought at a price."

Then pray, thanking God that he paid the price—a price we could never earn—to redeem us from bondage to sin. Thank him for the privilege of joining in his great plan of redemption as his slaves, serving him with all our heart, soul, and strength. Pray that those who are in bondage to sin will come to know Jesus and be set free from the power of darkness.

Memorize

> *Do you not know that . . . you are not your own; you were bought at a price.*
>
> *1 Corinthians 6:19–20*

The Gospel of Christ Provokes Imperial Rome

In-Depth Personal Study Sessions

Study One | God's Kingdom Brings a Different View of Slavery

The Very Words of God

> *Once when we were going to the place of prayer, we were met by a female slave who had a spirit by which she predicted the future. She earned a great deal of money for her owners by fortune-telling.*

Acts 16:16

Bible Discovery

Paul Encounters a Young Slave Girl

The book of Acts, Luke's record of Paul's travels, includes a number of "chance" meetings with people who significantly impacted his mission and, in a broader sense, the mission God has given to everyone who follows Jesus. First, as Paul (Saul at the time) traveled to Damascus to destroy the community of Jesus, he encountered Jesus himself. Then Ananias confirmed the mission Jesus gave to Paul. Next, Barnabas showed up and taught with Paul for a full year before they set out on what would become Paul's first teaching journey.

These, of course, were not chance meetings. In each one, God was at work. He had already provided the infrastructure of roads and a common language necessary to make the gospel of Christ known throughout the empire. Through each of these meetings, God was preparing the people who would be instrumental in demonstrating what the kingdom of heaven looked like on earth.

Luke, the Gentile doctor from Philippi who wrote the account of Paul's visit there, pointed out three encounters that had an impact on the gospel of Christ becoming known in that city (and eventually throughout the world even to this day). The first encounter was with Lydia. A wealthy Gentile God-fearer, she believed the good news and opened her heart, home, and resources to advance God's kingdom in Philippi. There was also the Philippian jailer who could not have imagined how the good news Paul brought to Philippi would change his life. In this study, we will focus on the unnamed slave girl whose encounter with Paul opens our eyes to the great battle that is being waged between the kingdom of heaven and the kingdom of the Evil One.

1. Following his custom of seeking out the Jewish community as his starting point for sharing the good news of Jesus, the Messiah, Paul and his companions were on their way to the place of prayer in Philippi when a young slave girl interrupted them. How disruptive was her communication about them, and what resulted? (See Acts 16:16–21.)

FOR GREATER UNDERSTANDING
How Could a Young Child Become a Slave?

As the Roman Empire grew, it became increasingly dependent on cheap slave labor. Slaves worked as domestics, street cleaners, masons, clerks, and tradesmen. If they had the skills, some served as artists, sculptors, musicians, or teachers. Lower-class slaves or those who had been convicted of crimes labored in the mines, galleys, and brothels where living conditions were deplorable. Some slaves were forced to fight in the games in the arenas. How did children, even very young children, become caught up in a life of slavery? There were several ways.

During the early years of the Roman Empire, most slaves were prisoners of war, and their families who were sold to pay the Roman soldiers. These families had children and often continued to have children while they were slaves. So by Paul's time, children had been born into slavery for generations. Slave owners owned their slaves' children just as they owned the offspring of their livestock, so it was customary for an owner to sell his slaves' children to a slave merchant. In turn, the slave merchant would train the children in some skill and sell them again. In other cases, slave owners kept attractive young women as well as young girls and boys for themselves in order to satisfy their own sexual appetites. In addition, families who could not pay their debts might be forced into slavery or sell one of their children to pay those debts.

THIS SCULPTURE OF A YOUNG GIRL IS DISPLAYED IN THE MUSEUM OF DELPHI. IT IS A POIGNANT REMINDER OF THE SLAVE GIRL FROM WHOM PAUL EXORCISED A DEMON AT PHILIPPI. TO THINK THAT THE OWNERS OF SUCH A CHILD DEDICATED HER TO APOLLO SO THAT SHE COULD BE FILLED WITH A DEMON CALLED A PYTHON SPIRIT IN ORDER TO MAKE MONEY FROM HER FORTUNE-TELLING HIGHLIGHTS THE EVIL AND CHAOS OF THE KINGDOM OF THIS WORLD.

Another common pathway to slavery occurred when parents rejected their children at birth. It is hard to imagine, but it was acceptable for parents to choose whether or not they were going to raise a newborn child. A child who was sickly, handicapped, or simply unwanted was taken outside the city and left to die. In the wealthy classes, a newborn infant was placed at the father's feet in a ceremony called *sublatus*—picking up—and if the father did not pick up the child and order that it be cared for, it was taken out to die.[6]

Not all children who were rejected died, however. Often slave merchants or poorer individuals would "rescue" the healthier newborns and raise and train them in particular skills so that they could be sold or kept as household slaves, whichever was most advantageous for the owner.

2. We know little about the slave who followed Paul and his companions, shouting out her message as they sought to share the gospel in Philippi. We don't know how she came to be a slave, but we know that Luke described her using the Greek word *paidiske*, which typically meant a young slave girl, perhaps only six to eight years old.[7]

    We also know little about how the child was treated by her owners. Despite societal pressures against extreme abuse, slaves often were treated horribly. The first-century Roman philosopher Seneca wrote, "The poor slaves may not move their lips, even to speak. The rod suppresses the slightest murmur; even a chance sound, a cough, a sneeze or a hiccup, is met with the lash. They often stand all night, hungry and dumb."[8]

    a. Based on their response after Paul freed this young child from the spirit within her, how do you think her owners viewed her and may have treated her? (See Acts 16:16, 18–19.)

    b. Without Paul's intervention, what hope would this child have had of being free from her human slave owners or the spirit that also "owned" her—and who would care?

3. In contrast to their Roman neighbors, the Jewish community, as well as the God-fearers and followers of Jesus who worshiped God with them, had a different view of slaves and slavery. The Jews generally rejected slavery as unacceptable based on their understanding of the Torah, which taught that a Jew was a slave of God.[9] Their understanding also grew out of their experience as slaves in Egypt.

    a. After God delivered the Hebrews and called them to be his own people, he gave them the law so that they would know how to be his partners in redemption— to show who God was and what his kingdom looked like when it was lived out on earth. How did the law require God's people to treat others, and how do you think this perspective would affect one's view of slavery? (See Deuteronomy 15:12–18; 16:9–12; 24:14–22.)

    b. In the ancient world of the Hebrews, people such as the Egyptians believed themselves to be slaves of their gods, who were cruel, unpredictable, and had to be appeased through religious ritual. So when God set the Hebrews free, he not only set them free from slavery to the Egyptians but also slavery to their gods. When God took them as his own people—his children and his bride—it was their honor and privilege to serve him. God was a master who commanded his people, his slaves, to rest one day a week—a privilege no other slave enjoyed. He created a legal code that protected them and ensured care for the poor, the widowed, and the orphan. As pointed out in Leviticus 25:55, God's people were to be slaves of no one "for the Israelites belong to me as servants. They are my servants, whom I brought out of Egypt. I am the Lord your God." In what ways does Paul reflect this principle in his instructions to followers of Jesus in 1 Corinthians 6:19–20; 7:21–23?

4. Apparently, slaves in the Roman world were allowed to choose which gods they would worship. Although temples were among the largest slave owners in the Roman Empire, slave participation in many of the ancient religions is widely attested. Many slaves also were receptive to the gospel message and its promise of redemption, eternal life, and restoration to God and his community of people. What bold claim did Paul make in Galatians 3:26–29 that is also emphasized in 1 Corinthians 12:13, Ephesians 6:8, and Colossians 3:11?

How do you think this statement would have been received by Roman society that clearly divided people into classes and granted respect, privilege, and opportunity accordingly? How might the young girl's owners have responded?

How do you think this statement would have been received by the underclass, the slaves who lived without justice in crushing poverty and suffering?

5. Although Paul's teaching about slavery in effect made owning slaves impossible for those who followed Jesus, he did not address the institution of slavery directly. Instead, how did he instruct both slaves and slave owners to behave in relationship to one another? (See Ephesians 6:5–9; Colossians 3:22–24; 4:1; 1 Timothy 6:1–2; Titus 2:9, 11.)

If Jesus-following slaves and masters lived according to these instructions, what impact would you expect them to have on the growing community of believers and its influence on Roman society, including the young slave girl's owners?

Reflection

The young girl Paul met in Philippi was twice a slave: owned by her masters who used her for their benefit and possessed by a python spirit. By the power of the name of Jesus, Paul set her free from enslavement to the demonic spirit. But Luke does not tell us what happened to the slave girl after Paul delivered her.

We don't know if the community of Jesus followers in Philippi bought her freedom once she was no longer profitable to her owners. We don't know if she found true freedom by choosing to be a slave of Jesus who died and rose again to pay the price for her redemption.

Apparently, Luke's primary intent was for us to realize that God bound the spirit of the strong man in Philippi just as Jesus had done in Galilee years earlier.[10] Jesus drove out demons and was accused of doing so through Satan's power. He rejected this opinion by pointing out that the Evil One, the one he called the "strong man," cannot rule a kingdom in conflict with his own. By driving out the demons, Jesus was taking away what the strong man claimed. "This can be done only," Jesus declared, "when the strong man is bound."

Paul came to Philippi with the good news that the kingdom of God has come! Since God had bound the strong man, the Evil One cannot keep those who have the freedom to be God's slaves from reclaiming what rightfully belongs to God! God's redemption brings *shalom*—peace, healing, and restoration to all who are enslaved by the Evil One.

> How much do you want to be part of God's work of redemption in your world?

> My heart goes out to that young child, and I ask myself, "What is my responsibility to set free the 'young slave girls' I encounter who are owned, possessed, and enslaved to the brutal gods of our culture?" How would you answer this question?

By our example, our prayers, our compassion, and the power of his name, God sets people free today just as he did in Galilee and Philippi. Being a slave of Christ puts us in a position to deliver others from bondage that they cannot escape on their own. How great a price are you willing to pay to identify yourself, as others have before you, as a "slave of Christ Jesus" (Philippians 1:1, "servant" in NIV) in order to set free those who are in bondage to the Evil One?

Study Two | Held Captive by a Python Spirit

The Very Words of God

Finally Paul became so annoyed that he turned around and said to the spirit, "In the name of Jesus Christ I command you to come out of her!" At that moment the spirit left her. When her owners realized that their hope of making money was gone, they seized Paul and Silas and dragged them into the marketplace to face the authorities.

Acts 16:18–19

Bible Discovery

God's Kingdom Responds with Great Power

When Paul and his companions brought the news of God's kingdom to Philippi, they must have known that tension would arise between the gospel they taught and the imperial gospel of the Roman colony. And it wasn't long before Paul's interaction with a young slave girl erupted into conflict. Although Imperial Rome played a role in the confrontation that ensued, it was not the source of opposition. The true source was the kingdom that has been in conflict with God since creation: the kingdom of Satan.

As Paul knew from the Scriptures, Satan's kingdom has actively opposed the advancement of God's kingdom throughout history. That kingdom and its demonic agents have brought destruction and chaos to God's creation. That kingdom strives to prevent God's people from experiencing his *shalom* and sharing it with others who are desperate for redemption and restoration to God's *beth ab*. That kingdom often opposed Jesus during his life and ministry—from his testing in the desert to the frequent appearance of demons among the people he taught. That kingdom will not relinquish to God's kingdom one inch of territory or one human heart without a battle.

In Philippi, Satan's kingdom of chaos made its appearance known through the seemingly harmless person of a young slave girl. Paul's interaction with her gives us a glimpse into the real battle taking place behind the scenes. Beneath the child's innocence was an evil spirit of great power that was determined to protect and expand Satan's kingdom of darkness. When Paul arrived and began presenting the light of God's kingdom in word and action, the war was on.

1. While Paul and his companions went about doing God's work in Philippi, they were followed by a young slave girl who shouted, "These men are servants of the Most High God, who are telling you the way to be saved"[11] (Acts 16:17). Luke's account goes on to say that she repeated her message for "many days" until Paul commanded the spirit to leave her (Acts 16:18). At first glance, it might seem to us that the child was making a true statement, but what might people in Philippi have heard in her words? Was she speaking the truth, or was her message deceptive? Consider the possibilities.

    a. Although the girl's proclamation sounded much like Paul's message, how did he respond to it? (See Acts 16:17–18.)

b. Who did Paul take action against—the girl or the spirit within her—and what does this indicate about the source and intent of her behavior?

c. Why do you think the source of the slave girl's message would be significant to Paul?

d. Was the girl's message conveying truth or chaos? Consider her statements in Acts 16:17 and how they would be understood by most Roman citizens in Philippi. Then write out how Paul would want his audience to understand them in light of Scripture.

The slave girl's statements	How the Roman world would understand her	Paul's intended meaning of such statements in light of Scripture
Most High God	In Philippi, "Most High God" would have referred to Jupiter or the emperor, not to the Lord Jesus.	See Genesis 14:18–22; Daniel 5:18–21.
Way to be saved	*Odon soterias* means "way of salvation," which, in the pluralistic world of the Roman Empire, would mean one among many ways to be saved.	See John 10:7–9; 14:6; Acts 2:21; 4:10–12; Romans 10:9–13.
Saved	References to the emperor or a god as "savior" or "one who saves" were commonly used in relation to deliverance from everyday problems such as poverty, illness, drought, etc. There was no concept of salvation through forgiveness of sin that resulted in eternal life.	See Luke 1:68–79; Mark 16:16; Acts 16:29–33; Ephesians 2:8–9.

DID YOU KNOW?
The Slave Girl Had a Python Spirit

The Greek text says the slave girl had a *pneuma python*, meaning a "python spirit," that enabled her to predict the future. That identification makes little sense to people today, but to Luke's readers it must have been startling. The ancients believed that a great python once guarded the sacred site at Delphi where the fertility goddess, Gaia, was venerated. In revenge for the python's attempted rape of his mother, Apollo killed the python and took over the shrine for himself.

A key feature of the shrine was the belief that when Apollo killed the python, it fell into an underground cavern where fumes from its decomposing body were released through an opening in the earth. When inhaled by a chosen priestess (called a *Pythia*) who served in the Apollo temple, those intoxicating vapors were said to allow the spirit of Apollo to possess her and enable her to speak ecstatic prophecies on his behalf. In a trance induced by the vapors, the Pythia became the voice of the gods, revealing their will and advising people on matters large and small. Thus the Oracle of Delphi became the most powerful woman in the ancient world.[12]

There is some science behind the ancient myth. The sacred site of Delphi is located over an intersection of geographic faults and underground caverns. It is believed that a natural gas pocket high in ethylene, which is known to produce violent trances, released fumes through an opening in the earth until a massive earthquake sealed it off in the fourth century AD.[13]

In Paul's day, the popularity of seeking oracles at Delphi for political matters had faded, but people still consulted the oracle for personal advice. A person who was possessed by a python spirit was thought to be inspired by Apollo and able to predict the future as he was. It is likely that the young slave girl had been taken to Delphi or another Apollo shrine to be dedicated to Apollo and filled with the python spirit. She then had trances and ecstatic experiences through the influence of that spirit, which her owners interpreted for their own economic gain. Examples of young girls who were possessed in this manner were known in the Roman world. It seems that this is Luke's understanding of the girl's spirit because he says she made a great deal of money for her masters by fortune-telling.

2. Unlike the Jews who had the written Word of God, the
    Greeks and Romans had no sacred texts. They were
    hungry for a word from their gods and longed for divine
    guidance for the future. So they sought to manipulate
    favor from their gods through sacrifices and offerings and
    viewed omens and oracles with high regard. In their view,
    the Pythia, the woman who was the Oracle of Delphi,
    literally was the voice of god. But ordinary people often
    did not have the means to travel to Delphi and seek an
    oracle from Apollo, so a child who was believed to have a
    python spirit that linked her to the god and gave her the
    ability to predict the future would be in high demand. In
    contrast, what does God say about his Word and the role
    it is to have in the lives of those who follow him? (See
    Romans 3:2; 15:4; 2 Timothy 3:16–17; Hebrews 4:12.)

3. The city of Ephesus, where Paul spent considerable time,
    was known for having significant demonic influence.
    What insight does Ephesians 2:1–6 provide into Paul's
    understanding of what it is like for a person to live under
    the influence of demons and in bondage to the "ways of
    this world," which is Satan's kingdom?

    How is it possible to escape such a life?

4. Acts 16:18 tells us that Paul became so "annoyed" by the young slave's harassment that he cast the spirit out of her. We must realize that being "annoyed" does not mean Paul was having a bad day or was reacting to a petty irritation. The word Luke used has the implication of being "deeply troubled" as well as annoyed.[14] It is translated in some versions as "grieved" and implies that Paul was struggling with deep inner pain.

   a. How do you think the girl's constant presence and shouting would have affected Paul's ability to find an audience and share the good news of Jesus as he walked through Philippi, and why would this have troubled him?

   b. Paul's mission was to make God's name known—to display God's character and increase his reputation so that people who did not know him would be drawn to him. Yet the publicity generated by the demonic spirit that possessed the girl was the opposite of his intent. How deeply must the demon's power and influence have troubled Paul, and why was it necessary for him to demonstrate God's power over the demon? (For a greater understanding of the power struggle between demons and God's kingdom and its influence on making God's name known, read what happened in Ephesus, Acts 19:11–20.)

c. It is hard to imagine a powerful demon, an agent of Satan's evil kingdom, possessing a young and helpless child. What about her situation and condition do you think deeply grieved Paul? (See Deuteronomy 24:17–22; Ephesians 4:32; Philippians 2:1–5; Colossians 3:12.)

FOR GREATER UNDERSTANDING
The Spiritual Battle Is Real

To the modern reader, it may seem that the account of the slave girl being possessed by the spirit of a pagan god is more ancient superstition and myth than reality. But the writers of the Text and their original audience believed differently. From the very beginning, the Text describes a great conflict between the Lord and an evil figure known as Satan. Satan appeared in the Garden of Eden (Genesis 3:1–5). The Jewish sages identified him as the rebellious one who was thrown out of heaven (Isaiah 14:12–13). Satan's objective is to destroy the *shalom* of God's creation, and he is the power behind every kind of evil in the world—hatred, immorality, injustice, oppression, and violence.

The idea of opposing kingdoms portrayed in the Bible—good against evil, God against Satan—comes from the ancient understanding of a "kingdom" as being anywhere a king's will is done. Thus Satan's kingdom, often referred to as the kingdom of this world, is defined as situations in which his will is done. His will is often carried out by evil powers known as demons who are believed to be fallen angels. In contrast, God's kingdom—the kingdom of heaven—is anywhere God's will is done.

The Hebrew Text calls God's people to join him in the struggle against the kingdom of this world by living in obedient service to God as their King and advancing the interests of the kingdom of heaven. The Christian Text portrays the conflict between the two kingdoms in the same way, providing additional detail about the work of Satan and his demonic forces.

Reflection

In different ways and on many occasions, Paul and the other apostles instructed followers of Jesus to become like him in every way. Following Jesus is not simply knowing about Jesus; it is total devotion to becoming like Jesus and a faithful commitment to live as he lived.

When he heard the cry of the hurting or saw a person suffering, Jesus was deeply troubled and moved to action. Time after time he restored God's *shalom* to the person and situation before him. As Jesus would have done, Paul also heard more than a shouting demon in the slave girl's inhuman cries. He heard a young child's cry for help, and his heart was deeply troubled and grieved. He understood that she was a tool in bondage to Satan and at the same time a child of God who needed to be rescued.

How might we have reacted to the disturbing shouts of the slave girl? Would we have shouted back? Turned away? Mocked her for her strange behavior? Posted nasty comments on her Facebook page? Or have we trained our ears to hear the call for help that Paul heard in her disturbing cries?

We can learn much from this story about being salt and light in our broken world. The Bible is clear. We have a mission to communicate through words and action who God is and what life looks like when his kingdom reigns.

So what do we hear when we recognize the demands of the complainer, the hate-filled screams of the accuser, the tirades of the angry, the demeaning mockery of the critic?

> Can you still hear in those who annoy and aggravate you a cry for help? Or has our loud, insensitive culture hardened your heart to their cries?

Do you choose to see in those with whom you disagree—and even in those who are completely evil—the image of God in a person being held hostage by the enemy?

What are you doing to "tune your ears" to hear the cry for help that Jesus hears, and to be so deeply moved that you act to make God's kingdom known in this broken, suffering world?

In what ways, without compromising with evil or shouting back at those who oppose you, will you demonstrate the love, compassion, forgiveness, and hope of the kingdom of heaven?

Study Three | Binding the Strong Man

The Very Words of God

Therefore God exalted him to the highest place and gave him the name that is above every name, that at the name of Jesus every knee should bow, in heaven and on earth and under the earth, and every tongue acknowledge that Jesus Christ is Lord, to the glory of God the Father.

Philippians 2:9–11

Bible Discovery

This World Belongs to God!

We live in a broken world, amidst a life-or-death conflict between the kingdom of heaven and the kingdom of this world. Satan remains a powerful king. His kingdom, the strong man's house, is real and present everywhere on earth. But make no mistake, this world—all of it—belongs to God. It does not belong to any other king, power, dominion, or name. And it certainly does not belong to Satan.

Jesus came to bring redemption and restoration to God's world. He came to bind the strong man, to break the power of Satan's grip on the people and institutions of this world, and to extend God's kingdom and reign to every corner of the earth. Following the example of his Lord and Savior, Paul walked into Philippi to bind the strong man and reclaim for the kingdom of heaven those who were in bondage to the kingdom of this world and rightfully belonged to God. There is much we can learn from the manner in which Jesus and Paul carried out their mission.

1. When you read the story of Paul's encounter with the slave girl who was possessed by a python spirit (Acts 16:16–19), what are your thoughts? Are you inclined to view it as more myth than reality? Does it seem far removed from what you understand your mission to be as a follower of Jesus? Do you have questions or fears about how you might face the powers of evil?

2. The Bible is clear that the battle between the kingdom of this world and the kingdom of heaven is real, and that as God's partners in redemption we struggle against a deceitful and powerful enemy. Consider how Jesus handled the inevitable conflicts with the kingdom of Satan.

a. From the moment his ministry began, who did Jesus confront, under whose leading, and what was the result? (See Matthew 4:1–11.)

b. Despite accusations to the contrary, by what power did Jesus battle the forces of the kingdom of Satan? (See Matthew 12:22–28.)

c. What did Jesus say is necessary in order to take back what Satan has stolen from God's kingdom? (See Matthew 12:29; Luke 11:21–22.[15])

d. What did Jesus do that ultimately defeated Satan's kingdom and his demonic forces? (See Colossians 2:13–15.)

3. What power did Jesus convey to his followers, and what was the result? (See Matthew 10:1, 5–8; Mark 6:7–13; Luke 10:1, 17–21.)

4. When Paul finally dealt with the slave girl's shouting, who did he address and by whose authority did he force the spirit to leave? (See Acts 16:17–18.)

Who was the real enemy in this encounter?

Who had the real authority and power in this encounter, and why? (See Philippians 2:9–11.)

5. As the early followers of Jesus accepted God's reign in their lives and carried out the mission to make God's name known, what happened in Jerusalem and Judea, then in Samaria, and then in places where Paul took the

gospel message that showed that God's kingdom had come and had overcome the power of the Evil One? (See Acts 5:12–16; 8:4–8; 19:11–20.)

How did people respond to what they witnessed?

How did they respond to the gospel of Jesus?

6. It is exciting to see the power of God at work in our broken world. When Jesus cast out demons, people were amazed. The only time the Bible describes Jesus as joyful occurred when he sent the disciples out to announce the kingdom of God, and they returned with the thrilling news that the demons submitted to them on the authority of his name. But in the excitement, we must not lose sight of who the real enemy is. Our battle is not against people or institutions, even though they may be evil. The battle is always against Satan and his demons. Read the following passages that provide examples of Jesus in action as he extended the kingdom of heaven and confronted the kingdom of Satan. (See Matthew 9:35–38; 14:13–20; 15:21–28; Mark 9:14–27; 10:46–52; Luke 4:31–37; 8:26–35.)

a. Which characteristics of Jesus do you notice in his interactions with people, and why is it necessary that we demonstrate those same qualities as we live out our God-given mission?

b. Which needs or priorities are most important for us to keep in perspective if we are to successfully demonstrate God's great love while also confronting the kingdom of Satan?

DID YOU KNOW?
The Strong Man Knows It Is Finished

For nearly 2,000 years, except during the winter months when Apollo was considered to be absent, the Oracle of Apollo at Delphi spoke on behalf of the gods to pagan people who sought her wisdom and advice. People from around the Mediterranean world made their way to the temple complex on Mount Parnassus in central Greece. Usually they came by boat to the harbor city of Kirrha on the Gulf of Corinth, then began the 10-mile, 2,500-foot climb to Delphi.

On the seventh day after the new moon—the sacred day of Apollo—pilgrims would purify themselves at the Kastalia spring, offer sacrifices at the temple of Athena, then line up along the sacred way, hoping for a chance to make their inquiries. Of course, seeking pilgrims were placed in line according to their status and wealth. Cities and those who could afford it paid tremen-

dous fees to be placed at the front of the line while ordinary people were placed farther back, hoping they would make it to the temple in time.

Meanwhile, the Pythia, the high priestess of Apollo, also was purified at the spring and offered a goat sacrifice in front of the Apollo temple. She then descended into the crypt beneath the temple where she sat on a tripod and inhaled the vapors that rose through a crevice beneath her. The Oracle at Delphi was unusual because pilgrims were allowed into the temple, into the holy of holies, and down into a chamber near where the Pythia sat so that they could ask her their questions. In a deep, raspy voice she would utter cryptic, poetic phrases that a male priest would write down and interpret for the inquirer.

The Pythia's utterings were taken very seriously. King Croesus of Sardis and the Athenians as well as others are known to have consulted her regarding their war strategies. In fact, the Athenians' strategy for the great sea battle of Marathon when the Greeks defeated the Persians is said to have come from her oracle. Those who had the means left behind gifts to thank Apollo for the oracle that had benefitted them. Over time, Delphi became the richest of all the sanctuaries in Greece. "Treasuries" or small temples to hold trophies and gifts lined the sacred way from the gate of the sacred enclosure up to the temple itself.

But the power behind the oracle was none other than Satan. For that reason, the early Church Fathers cautioned against any involvement with the oracle or the Pythia. And as the gospel of Christ became known and the community of Jesus followers extended the influence of God's kingdom, the importance of the oracle declined. Even so, the kingdom of Satan did not surrender easily. In 303 AD, Emperor Diocletian consulted another ancient oracle of Apollo at Didyma, and she said that the revelation of Apollo was being hindered by "the just on earth." Diocletian interpreted "the just on earth" to mean the followers of Jesus. So he launched a severe persecution of believers throughout the Roman Empire.

But the kingdom of God continued to grow in numbers and influence, reclaiming lives that Satan had held in bondage. In about 380 AD, the Christian emperor Theodosius I destroyed the temple of Apollo at Delphi. According to tradition, ten or so years later, the Pythia spoke her last oracle: "Tell the king the fair-wrought house has fallen. No shelter has Apollo. The fountains are now silent. The voice is still. It is finished."

By the greater power that hung on a cross and cried out, "It is finished," the strong man was bound. God's kingdom will prevail. The Evil One knows he is finished, but he will not relinquish his kingdom without a fight.

Reflection

When Paul, armed by the power of Jesus' name, forced the demon to leave the little slave girl, he was fulfilling the mission that Jesus has passed on to all who follow him. Satan's kingdom was diminished, and God's kingdom expanded! But the strong man does not give up his kingdom without opposition.

Yes, the power of Jesus is greater than the power of Satan. Yes, the strong man is defeated. But he is not yet destroyed. That will come. Until then, the battle wages on.

When Paul took back one child for God's kingdom, the Evil One and those who remained in his service were not pleased. When the spirit left the girl, so did her owners' profit. Acts 16:19–21 reveals their vehement response:

> *When her owners realized that their hope of making money was gone, they seized Paul and Silas and dragged them into the marketplace to face the authorities. They brought them before the magistrates and said, "These men are Jews, and are throwing our city into an uproar by advocating customs unlawful for us Romans to accept or practice."*

What would happen to Paul and Silas? We will explore the outcome of this incident in our next study. But there is one more thought we need to take to heart as we consider our role in taking back for God's kingdom that which Satan has claimed as his own.

The slave owners' response to losing their ability to make money should not surprise us. It is almost instinctive that people become less compassionate and less sensitive to using others for their own benefit when their financial status is threatened. Sadly, even in the community of Jesus we are inclined to protect ourselves from those in need if we fear that our own self-interests might suffer.

Although we seldom are confronted by someone who is demon possessed, we live in a world of two kingdoms and are enticed by the self-serving interests of the kingdom of the Evil One every day. Our own loyalty is divided as we sometimes obey the Lord our King and at other times succumb to the seductive influence of the Evil One. Instead of walking in the ways of God and living as Jesus lived, we choose for self and ignore the needs of others. Security, pleasure, materialism, and leisure overrule our commitment to bring the gospel of restoration, healing, and hope to a broken world.

> The gospel is likely to meet opposition whenever it threatens economic interests. So the question for each of us who would follow Jesus is: "Is that true of me as well? In what ways does the gospel meet opposition from the self-interests of my heart?"

Jesus sacrificed himself for others—for each of us who were sinners in helpless bondage to the kingdom of Satan. He put aside his own needs for the benefit of others in the way he lived and died. How far will you go to be like Jesus so that others will see what the kingdom of heaven looks like when it reigns on earth?

Knowing the self-serving attitudes of the Hellenistic society in which he lived, Paul wrote, "Do nothing out of selfish ambition or vain conceit. Rather, in humility value others above yourselves, not looking to your own interests but each of you to the interests of others. In your relationships with one another, have the same mindset as Christ Jesus" (Philippians 2:3–5). So one day in Philippi, not knowing what it might cost him, Paul took back a child in the name of Jesus. Will you do the same? Whose interests will you value more highly than your own?

THE PHILIPPIAN JAILER

The good news that Jesus is Savior and Lord was never meant to be simply a religious message. Being a living example of God's character and ways has always been God's calling for his people. Based on the redeeming work of Jesus, the gospel calls those who follow him not only to teach God's ways but to demonstrate them in every life activity—whether it be politics, family life, social relationships, cultural practices, or business. The gospel of Christ demands compassion for those who suffer, obedient submission to the will of God, recognition of every person as a valuable individual created in the image of God, and sacrifice of oneself in order to serve the interests of others. In the Roman world, such a lifestyle would not go unnoticed. The daily life priorities for citizens of God's kingdom were diametrically opposed to the Hellenistic priorities of the Roman way.

In Philippi, some people who had experienced life's chaos and lived apart from God, not even knowing who he was, responded to the good news eagerly. The poor, the diseased, the slaves, the lonely, the oppressed, and the marginalized recognized that the kingdom of heaven Paul proclaimed was very different from the kingdom that ruled their world. In the kingdom of heaven, which was put on display for them by the believers in Philippi, they were loved, cared for, and treated with dignity. There was no division of slave or free, rich or poor, male or female, Jew or Gentile. Imagine that! All were one in Messiah and shared with others as each had a need.

Some accepted the truth of Paul's message and immediately joined the mission as God's partners in restoring *shalom* and extending his reign in their community. They opened their homes and invited others to join them in the same way the first believers had that day in Jerusalem when God's Spirit came upon them on Pentecost.[1] In just a short time, a community of people came to know Jesus and joined the mission. As a community, they established a colony of heaven in Philippi and began presenting his gospel to a dark and broken culture. But not everyone was pleased.

Paul's message that the God of Israel was Savior and Lord and that his kingdom had come was very unsettling for some people. After all, the gospel of the kingdom of heaven has implications for every aspect of life. Trouble came from the wealthy and powerful who were comfortable with the system as it was because it benefitted them greatly. So it should not surprise us that the first sign of trouble was not over a religious issue in the strict sense, but an economic matter. The people of Philippi discovered what the city of Thessalonica would soon learn as well: "These men who have turned the world upside down have come here also" (Acts 17:6 ESV). That clash of kingdoms—so clearly demonstrated when the message of the kingdom of heaven is lived out in daily life and stands in sharp contrast to the lifestyle of the kingdom of this world—is the focus of this study.

Opening Thoughts (3 minutes)

The Very Words of God

> *"Believe in the Lord Jesus, and you will be saved—you and your household." Then they spoke the word of the Lord to him and to all the others in his house. At that hour of the night the jailer took them and washed their wounds; then immediately he and all his household were baptized. The jailer brought them into his house and set a meal before them; he was filled with joy because he had come to believe in God—he and his whole household.*

> *Acts 16:31–34*

Think About It

All of us face obstacles and challenges. Times when we have a plan to accomplish something we value greatly and things just don't go as we thought they were "supposed" to go. Times when we do what has always worked for us before, and it all goes wrong. Times when we successfully do the right thing, and it seems everyone hates us for it. Times when things go so "wrong" we don't even know what is happening!

In such situations, some people become hopelessly discouraged. Others give up. Some get angry. And some people are so committed and focused on the goal that they are energized by what stops others dead in their tracks!

What do you think accounts for the difference?

What motivates some people to keep the faith and expect great things to happen while others can't even face the obstacle(s), much less strive to overcome it (them)?

Video Notes (32 minutes)

Paul: citizen of Rome; citizen of heaven

Philippi: Roman in every way

Where the gospel of Caesar rules

Punishment Roman style

The Philippian jail

The price of being the message

Prayer and praise at midnight

Suddenly God shows up

The Philippian jailer: "What must I do to be saved?"

Validate the message

Video Discussion (7 minutes)

1. As modern Westerners, we don't often think of how our
    surroundings make cultural or political statements about
    our world. But in the Roman world a person couldn't go
    anywhere without seeing "monuments" of all sorts that
    were reminders of the "gospel" of Rome. Discuss the cul-
    tural and political messages that would be conveyed to a
    person who simply walked through the Roman colony of
    Philippi, particularly through the forum, the heart of the
    city where much of this video was filmed. To help remem-
    ber some of these locations, refer to the map of Philippi
    on page 156.

- The *Via Egnatia*—the Roman road next to the forum that stretched across ancient Macedonia from Byzantium to Dyrrhacium on the Adriatic Sea, then across the sea to the Appian Way that led to Rome.

- The Greek theater where the Roman games were held.

- The forum, where people gathered to exchange goods and ideas.

- The imperial temple with its huge, fluted columns.

- The imperial altar, set up for the veneration and worship of the emperor.

- The *bema*, where magistrates gave official pronouncements and passed judgments.

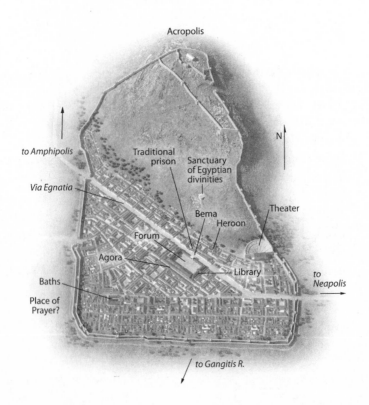

THE REMAINS OF THE IMPERIAL TEMPLE IN THE FORUM OF PHILIPPI

2. If we understand that in the Jewish mind "prayer" encompassed far more than just petition—but also worship, recitation of the Text, and singing—how does that inform our understanding of how Paul and Silas handled their imprisonment?

In what ways did their attitudes and responses toward the injustice, pain, and uncertainty of their imprisonment differ from what ours might have been?

What do you think enabled Paul and Silas to approach their horrific circumstances as they did?

3. The story of Paul, Silas, and the Philippian jailer is non-stop drama of tremendous consequence—the late-night earthquake, the release without escape for the prisoners, the jailer's deliverance from suicide, the baptism of his household, attending to the wounds of Paul and Silas, the magistrates' sudden release of Paul and Silas, and Paul's claim to citizenship and insistence on honorable treatment from those who had abused him.

    a. How memorable do you think each of these events was in the minds of at least some of the people of Philippi?

    b. What impact might these events have had on how the gospel of Christ was received by specific people in Philippi—Roman soldiers and authorities, prisoners, slaves, Jesus followers, and others?

Small Group Bible Discovery and Discussion (13 minutes)

A Citizen of Two Worlds

As we've seen, Philippi was a Roman colony where Caesar reigned as lord. The Roman citizens who lived there recognized their exceptional privilege and were extremely loyal to Caesar's kingdom, the Roman Empire. Paul was uniquely qualified to bring the gospel of Jesus to this city because, as Luke informs us, he also was a Roman citizen, possessing all rights and privileges. Paul was one of them! His message would be heard and validated based, in part, on his status as a Roman citizen.

However, Paul apparently came to Philippi without making known his Roman citizenship. He must have dressed like a Jew and worn tassels,[2] as God had commanded, because the people of the city recognized him as a Jew. When trouble began, the enraged mob shouted, "These men are Jews" (Acts 16:20). Clearly Paul had not hidden his Jewish identity. He went into Philippi as a Jew and a follower of Jesus in order to continue to fulfill the mission God gave to his ancestors at Mount Sinai: "You will be for me a kingdom of priests and a holy nation" (see Exodus 19:2–6).

What did God mean when he called his people to be a kingdom of priests? In the ancient world, a priest's role was to demonstrate who God was and what he was like. And a kingdom was viewed as any situation in which a king reigned and people obeyed his will. So when God graciously redeemed Israel and commissioned them to be his kingdom of priests, he gave them the mission of displaying his character and ways so that people would come to know him. By obeying God's will in all aspects of life, his people would be, in effect, citizens of heaven who would extend his rule and his kingdom wherever they were. Whenever God's people obediently live out his will, God reigns and, as Jesus said, his kingdom comes on earth as it is in heaven (Matthew 6:10).

When Paul came to Philippi, he came not as a Roman citizen representing the kingdom and ways of this world but as a citizen of God's kingdom demonstrating what life is like when God is in control. It is not at all surprising that conflict would occur as Paul proclaimed and lived out the gospel message. The kingdom of heaven and the kingdom of this world are always in opposition. What is surprising is that Paul does not reveal his Roman citizenship until he is ready to leave the city. He did not use the advantage that his status as a Roman citizen gave him even though doing so would have saved him from a great deal of personal suffering.

The fact that Paul didn't play his Roman citizenship card is surprising because he usually made use of every available situation to generate greater interest in his message. He wrote to the believers in Corinth, "I have become all things to all people so that by all possible means I might save some. I do all this for the sake of the gospel" (1 Corinthians 9:22–23). Why would he choose to hide his citizenship in a city filled with Roman citizens? If on other occasions he used the privileges his citizenship gave him to protect himself and enhance his opportunities to be heard, why not in Philippi?

1. Paul was born a Jew in the city of Tarsus, a wealthy commercial center of the Gentile world. For at least some of his early years, his family lived in the context of the social, educational, financial, philosophical, and moral values of the Roman world. But his family were Pharisees, so they would have been devoted to righteous living in obedience to Torah. Paul took his heritage and calling as a Jew very seriously. In what ways do we know he was a "citizen" of the kingdom of heaven as the Jews of his day understood it? Make a list! (See Exodus 19:3–6; Deuteronomy 5:32–33; 6:4–5; Acts 22:3–5; 2 Corinthians 11:22; Philippians 3:3–6.)

2. What other citizenship did Paul rightfully claim that was very important in the world in which he lived? (See Acts 22:24–28.)

DID YOU KNOW?
How Paul Became a Roman Citizen

Luke's account of Paul's ministry reveals that Paul was born a Roman citizen (Acts 22:28), which was unusual for a Jew. Although Luke doesn't reveal how Paul's family became citizens, the writings of Jerome, one of the great Church Fathers (342–420 AD), offer a plausible explanation. Jerome lived in Israel and named Gischala in northern Galilee as the hometown of Paul's parents. Apparently, his parents participated in a revolt against Rome, were captured, and subsequently were sold as slaves to a Roman citizen in Tarsus. Later they were freed, becoming Roman citizens, which enabled their son to be a Roman citizen as well.[3]

Legitimate children of Roman citizens were required to be registered within thirty days of birth. The child's name was entered on the register in that province, and a *testatio*, a document not unlike a birth certificate, provided proof of the child's citizenship. A person would normally keep the *testatio* in a small wooden tablet called a *diptych*.[4] We do not know whether Paul carried such a document with him, but the penalty for making a false claim of Roman citizenship was severe. Because the Roman authorities apparently did not question Paul's citizenship, it is likely he was able to show some evidence for his claim.

3. Paul knew that as a Jew he was called to a life of obedience to God's commands in order to fulfill his priestly mission of making God known to his world. After Jesus met Paul on the road to Damascus, what specific instructions did Paul receive regarding how he was to fulfill the mission? (See Acts 22:21.)

How did Paul view his role in fulfilling the mission? (See Romans 15:15–19.)

In what ways do you think Paul's citizenship in two kingdoms—the kingdom of heaven as a Jew and a follower of Jesus, and the kingdom of Rome as a Roman citizen—prepared him for the mission?

4. What events unfolded in Philippi (Acts 16:16–22) that illustrate the deep rift between the kingdom of Rome (the kingdom of this world) and the kingdom of heaven (the kingdom of God)?

Do you think Paul and Silas anticipated that something like this might happen? Why or why not?

What issue caused the uproar? Was it what Paul said and taught or how he put God on display through his actions?

In what ways is the "citizenship" of the parties involved—the slave owners, Paul, the mob, the magistrates—evident in this interaction?

Faith Lesson (4 minutes)

Paul was keenly aware that he was a citizen of two worlds: the world's kingdom of Rome and God's kingdom of heaven. But his citizenship in the kingdom of heaven—his allegiance to the laws and customs of heaven itself—determined how he lived as a citizen in this world. When his Roman citizenship enhanced his opportunities to proclaim Jesus as Messiah, Paul used that advantage, but not at the expense of his calling as a citizen of heaven.

For followers of Jesus then as well as now, citizenship in God's kingdom must always be first. Our authority as ambassadors of God's kingdom is validated by how we live—how we put God on display as we do his will every day. As one historian has observed, "The new believers were attracted to the community of Jesus' followers first. Only then did they begin to realize they were attracted to the person of Jesus."[5]

In a letter from an early believer named Mathetes to Diognetus, we see a powerful description of how Christians lived as citizens of heaven during the late first and early second centuries:

Christians are not distinguished from other men by country, language, nor by the customs that they observe. They do not inhabit cities of their own, use a particular way of speaking, nor lead a life marked out by any curiosity. The course of conduct they follow has not been devised by the speculation and deliberation of inquisitive men. They do not, like some, proclaim themselves the advocates of merely human doctrines.

Instead, they inhabit both Greek and barbarian cities, however things have fallen to each of them. And it is while following the customs of the natives in clothing, food, and the rest of ordinary life that they display to us their wonderful and admittedly striking way of life.

They live in their own countries, but they do so as those who are just passing through. As citizens they participate in everything with others, yet they endure everything as if they were foreigners. Every foreign land is like their homeland to them, and every land of their birth is like a land of strangers.

They marry, like everyone else, and they have children, but they do not destroy their offspring.

They share a common table, but not a common bed.

They exist in the flesh, but they do not live by the flesh. They pass their days on earth, but they are citizens of heaven. They obey the prescribed laws, all the while surpassing the laws by their lives.

They love all men and are persecuted by all. They are unknown and condemned. They are put to death and restored to life.

They are poor, yet make many rich. They lack everything, yet they overflow in everything.

They are dishonored, and yet in their very dishonor they are glorified; they are spoken ill of and yet are justified; they are reviled but bless; they are insulted and repay the insult with honor; they do good, yet are punished as evildoers; when punished, they rejoice as if raised from the dead. They are assailed by the Jews as barbarians; they are persecuted by the Greeks; yet those who hate them are unable to give any reason for their hatred.[6]

These devoted believers were not known by what they said, but by how they lived! They were continuing the mission God had given to Israel, the mission Jesus lived and taught, the mission Paul brought to the Gentiles!

1. What about you? Do people recognize you as a citizen of heaven, or do they see more of the world's citizenship in your lifestyle and relationships?

2. Write out some important things that you think distinguish a citizen of heaven in your world. How will you put them into practice in your daily life and interaction with others, starting today?

Closing (1 minute)

Read 1 Peter 2:12 aloud together: "Live such good lives among the pagans that, though they accuse you of doing wrong, they may see your good deeds and glorify God on the day he visits us."

Then pray, thanking God that he not only has redeemed us but has made us his partners in redeeming others from bondage to the kingdom of this world. Ask for his forgiveness for the times we forget (or ignore) that we are citizens of his kingdom who have been given the privilege of serving him so that we might make him known to a world that desperately needs him. Ask him for wisdom, grace, and faithfulness to live good lives that bring glory, honor, and praise to his holy name.

Memorize

Live such good lives among the pagans that, though they accuse you of doing wrong, they may see your good deeds and glorify God on the day he visits us.

1 Peter 2:12

The Gospel of Christ Pr Imperial Rome

In-Depth Personal Study Sessions

Study One | Philippi Reacts to the Coming of God's Kingdom

The Very Words of God

They brought them before the magistrates and said, "These men are Jews, and are throwing our city into an uproar by advocating customs unlawful for us Romans to accept or practice."

Acts 16:20–21

Bible Discovery

Paul and Silas Create an "Uproar"

When Paul and Silas brought the gospel of Jesus to Philippi, they knew that what they *did* to display God's character was just as—or even more—important than what they *said*. Whether in Paul's day or ours, living according to the attitudes and priorities of Jesus shapes everything a follower of Jesus does. It affects our families, our businesses, our politics, our community relationships, our leisure, the way we use God's creation, how we treat others who are created in God's image, and how we respond to those who are marginalized.

A true presentation of the gospel of Jesus as Savior and Lord that is lived out in daily life will always have powerful repercussions in a world that clings to a different gospel—in this case the gospel of the Roman emperor who claimed to be lord and savior. It is not so much the message of the gospel but its implications that offend those who are not of the kingdom of heaven. Nowhere did this conflict occur more powerfully than when Roman power and law met the gospel of Jesus after a little slave irl's owners literally dragged Paul and Silas before the Roman authorities in Philippi.

To understand the conflict, we must realize that citizens in a Roman colony were very proud of being Roman. They were extremely protective of all customs and laws lest "foreigners"

undermine their ways, their worship, their cultural practices, and—most importantly—the privileges and prosperity they received from Rome. No colony was more loyal and devoted than Philippi, and its citizens had every reason to react against any circumstance that might undermine the good life they enjoyed.

Philippi was laid out like Rome itself. The main east-west street, the *Via Egnatia*, passed through the center of the city past the imperial temple and the forum. The *bema*, or judges' stand, was located on the side of the forum, as it is in the forum in Rome. More than eighty inscriptions found in the excavations of Philippi are in Latin even though the city is located in Greece. Temples were built in Roman style, and the ancient Greek theater was turned into an amphitheater for gladiatorial games. The Philippians also enjoyed running water and Roman baths, the kind of advantages Roman citizens would expect in a Roman colony.

So, it is not difficult to understand why Philippi's citizens were highly protective of their "Roman customs." They lived a good life. Their first loyalty was to country and culture. When Paul, who had the appearance of a Jew—a foreigner—started displaying the "customs" of the kingdom of heaven by delivering a young slave girl from bondage to a python spirit (which also

THE FORUM (LATIN), AGORA (GREEK), OR MARKETPLACE OF PHILIPPI. THE FORUM OF A ROMAN CITY WAS A LARGE PUBLIC-GATHERING PLACE—THE CENTER OF ATHLETIC, ARTISTIC, SPIRITUAL, COMMERCIAL, AND POLITICAL LIFE. IT WAS ALSO THE LOCATION WHERE OFFICIAL ANNOUNCEMENTS FROM THE EMPEROR OR HIS REPRESENTATIVES WERE MADE.

"delivered" her owners of their future income!), trouble erupted immediately. Paul and Silas quickly discovered just how intensely Philippi's citizens would protect their Roman gospel.

1. Living out the gospel of Christ risks—and virtually guarantees—conflict with all other gospels. Such clashes often are not focused on spiritual matters or religious practices but on political, cultural, or ideological matters. What action initiated the "uproar" Paul and Silas were accused of causing in Philippi? (See Acts 16:16–22.)

    In what ways was Paul's action in delivering the slave girl from the python spirit a true expression of the gospel of Christ?

In what ways did the slave owners' response express the character of the gospel of Rome?

Would you have expected Rome's response in Philippi to be as swift, powerful, and widespread as it was? Why or why not?

PROFILE OF A COLONY
A Life of Privilege in a Roman Colony

Colonies played an important role in Roman imperial expansion. The city of Rome had grown to more than one million people, one-third of them slaves, so unemployment was very high and little land was available. Colonies provided a place where Roman citizens could own land yet live as if they were in Rome. It was as if Roman soil had been transported to another country.

Equally important, colonies became beachheads for "Romanizing" the empire, for exerting influence on cultural practice and belief. If the empire was to be prosperous and united, the far-flung provinces must understand what it meant to be Roman and desire the Roman peace and its provision of power, wealth, pleasure, and leisure. Colonies often had significant populations of Roman soldiers who were a powerful influence for controlling local populations, making it possible to extend and secure the empire without war.

Colonies typically had greater resources than cities that were not colonies. Those who lived in a colony enjoyed significant infrastructure such as aqueducts for running water, paved roads, theaters, arenas, temples, and baths. In addition, religious practice was more "Roman" in a colony than in other cities. Because the emperor—who had absolute authority over the empire—was deemed to be the son of god, god and country were inseparable. Emperor worship was the central religious experience, and it was encouraged as a unifying element for everyone—citizen or not. The imperial cult sponsored games, plays, and religious festivals where sacrificial meat was distributed to the people. Honored on coins, inscriptions, and statues as the savior of the world, the emperor was responsible for all the benefits a colony enjoyed.

While other cities had some of these advantages, few could compare with the advantages of a colony. In addition, it all came with the promise of Roman protection of life and property. The emperor would protect them if any danger arose. So it is not surprising that the highest loyalty of a Roman citizen, particularly in a Roman colony, was the mother city: Rome.

2. When Paul, being a living example of the gospel message, delivered the slave girl from the spirit that possessed her, it affected her owners in the pocketbook. In fact, Luke makes a point of this in his original writing of the account (Acts 16:18–19). He writes that the spirit "left her," and then writes that the hope of making money "left them!" No wonder they became very angry. But this wasn't the only time the life-giving priorities of the gospel of Christ had, or would, threaten the insatiable desire for prosperity of the gospel of Rome. In each of the following situations, consider not only what occurred and its severity but the deeper nature of the conflict between the two gospels.

	Jesus in the Decapolis*	Paul in Ephesus	Paul in Philippi
The Text	*Mark 5:1–20*	*Acts 19:23–41*	*Acts 16:16–24*
What impact was the gospel having as it was being lived out in each community?			
Who perceived the gospel of the kingdom of heaven as a threat, and for what reason(s)?			
What concern did those who felt threatened by the implications of the gospel of Christ have for the people whose lives had been restored?			
How did people who were committed to the ways and benefits of the kingdom of this world respond to the conflict?			
What risk(s) did those who lived as citizens of heaven in this world face?			

*For further study on this interaction, please refer to That the World May Know, Vol.14, *The Mission of Jesus: Triumph of God's Kingdom in a World of Chaos*, session 2.

3. If Jesus is, as the prophets declared, *Lord* (see Isaiah 52:7; 61:1), then his gospel is not simply a religious truth or spiritual experience. It is a proclamation of ultimate reality that affects every part of life. If Jesus is Lord, and his kingdom comes as his will is done, then there are serious implications for that "other" kingdom when God's people live in obedience to his will. Why would this make the slave girl's owners and the Roman authorities—even Caesar—nervous?

4. One of the rights reserved for Roman citizens was the ability to own and benefit from private property (which included slaves) without interference from others. In what sense did Paul's deliverance of the slave girl violate her owners' rights, and what strong action did they take against Paul and Silas? (See Acts 16:19.)

FOR GREATER UNDERSTANDING
How Did They Know Paul Was a Jew?

In ancient times, the clothing people wore often revealed their identity and social status. The hem and tassels (Hebrew, *tzitzit*) of the outer robe were particularly important, symbolizing the owner's identity and authority. Those in the upper class—nobility, kings, and princes—decorated their hems with tassels.

God has always wanted his people to stand out as unique among the nations—morally, socially, economically, and religiously. He has always

wanted the community of his people to display him to the world and show what every activity of life looks like when God's kingdom reigns on earth. So in addition to other commands related to Jewish purity, identity, dress, diet, health, and social practices, he commanded them to wear tassels.[7] The tassels, which included a blue cord the color of the priests' garments, served as a constant reminder to obey God's commands always and to live in the world as his kingdom of priests.

The tassels reminded both Jews and Gentiles of the Jews' status as God's holy, chosen people.[8] As a Pharisee who was committed to obey all of God's commands fully, Paul would have worn tassels. The tassels and possibly other features of his clothing and the way his hair was cut would have identified him as a Jew rather than a Roman.

5. Roman citizens in a Roman colony had the right to make a "citizen's arrest" of foreigners who were believed to have threatened the peace of their city, which also would have been viewed as a direct threat to Rome and the entire Roman Empire. The slave girl's owners exercised this right for their advantage. To expand their grievance and make Paul's action a public offense—even though he had said nothing against the Roman Empire—which three charges did the slave owners bring against him? (See Acts 16:19–21.)

Consider why these charges were deemed detrimental to the security of the Roman colony of Philippi. First, although Roman law allowed Jews to practice their faith, there is evidence of strong anti-Semitism in the Roman Empire. Furthermore, Emperor Claudius had recently expelled all Jews from Rome for "disturbing the peace."[9]

What do you think the slave owners hoped to accomplish by making these charges against Paul and Silas?

Every cultural and religious practice in a Roman colony was carefully managed to maintain peace, stability, and devotion to Roman ways. The Romans were very concerned about anything that would offend or diminish the honor of their gods or emperor. How could the power Paul exercised over the spirit of Apollo when he drove out the demon from the slave girl be viewed as a threat?

THE *BEMA*, OR "JUDGES' BENCH" IN THE FORUM, OR MARKETPLACE OF PHILIPPI

6. When the slave girl's owners dragged Paul and Silas
   into the *agora*, or forum, to bring their charges before
   the magistrates, the incident immediately became public
   knowledge. It would be like something going viral today.
   Soon a mob gathered and joined in the attack, creating a
   very tense and volatile situation. When the official judgment that Paul's actions violated and undermined Roman
   law was made, what happened to Paul and Silas? (See
   Acts 16:20–23.)

Why do you think that even with this turn of events Paul
did not claim his Roman citizenship, which would have
eliminated the charges and spared him the severe flogging and imprisonment that followed?

Why do you think it is significant that this judgment was
made in a Roman colony and therefore represented the
authority of Imperial Rome—the emperor himself?

THINK ABOUT IT
How Different It Might Have Been

As a Roman citizen, Paul had the same rights and privileges as those who were demanding that their rights of Roman citizenship be upheld by punishing him. In contrast to a foreigner, a Roman citizen was exempt from scourging and had the right of appeal to the emperor's magistrate. Citizens had *immunitas*, meaning they were exempt from tribute and most forms of taxation. They had *dignitas*, meaning the right to receive honor from other citizens, especially from foreigners. They had *libertas*, or self-government. They had the right to take civil action to reclaim losses. And they enjoyed social and economic benefits such as subsidized bread and free games and performances.

Think about how differently this entire scene would have played out if Paul had claimed his Roman citizenship. Yet Paul willingly set aside all these protections and benefits in order to display the kingdom of heaven so that some might be saved!

7. Satan, ruler of the kingdom of this world, has claimed all of God's creation for himself; God is redeeming what Satan has stolen and restoring it to the kingdom of heaven. So these two kingdoms are incompatible. They cannot coexist without conflict. The kingdom of this world has and will always react when God's people serve him as their King and thereby extend his reign on earth.

   a. What did Jesus say that puts this conflict into perspective for those who become objects of hatred and persecution because they follow him and live out the gospel of God's kingdom? (See John 15:18–21.)

b. As Paul faced the challenges of planting a colony
    for Jesus in Philippi, which he had done in Antioch
    of Pisidia, Iconium, Lystra, and Derbe, what was the
    source of his hope and strength as the kingdom of
    heaven clashed with the kingdom of this world? (See
    Philippians 1:18–21; 2:13–17.)

Reflection

It is important for those of us who follow Jesus today to recognize what happened in Philippi because it is what we also must
expect if we are faithful to the mission God has called us. As
we declare to our culture what we believe and what God has
revealed, some will listen and also believe. But when we actually
obey God in every area of life and thereby demonstrate what life
looks like when God is in control, we become a living critique of
our culture. When our actions reveal compassion for those who
suffer (think of the slave girl), when the purity of our morality
can't be denied, when we show respect for all people (especially
those with whom we disagree or whose lifestyle we disapprove),
when we live as if Jesus and no other is Lord, it shakes the kingdom of this world to its foundation. And those who live by that
kingdom will oppose us—sometimes violently.

So, if we are not challenged or making sacrifices for what we
believe and how we live, we must carefully examine whether we
are faithful to God's call in our lives.

Paul was violently dragged into court and severely beaten for his
views and actions. Should we expect to live with no resistance to
our faith? No objections to our lifestyle? Why or why not?

What impact are you and other followers of Jesus in your community making by the way you live life every day?

Who feels threatened by the implications of how you live, and how are they responding?

If you really live as a citizen of heaven in this world, what risks do you face?

God certainly prepared Paul to fulfill his calling to *bring* and to *be* the gospel message in the Roman world. Paul wanted all followers of Jesus to be prepared to be a living demonstration of God's kingdom on earth and to be equipped for inevitable conflict with the kingdom of this world. In Ephesians 6:11–20, he instructs followers of Jesus in what it takes to be strong in the power of the Lord:

> *Put on the full armor of God, so that you can take your stand against the devil's schemes. For our struggle is not against flesh and blood, but against the rulers, against the authorities, against the powers of this dark world and against the spiritual forces of evil in the heavenly realms. Therefore put on the full armor of God, so that when the day of evil comes, you may be able to stand your ground, and after you have done everything, to stand. Stand firm then, with the belt of truth buckled around your waist, with the breastplate of righteousness in place,*

and with your feet fitted with the readiness that comes from the gospel of peace. In addition to all this, take up the shield of faith, with which you can extinguish all the flaming arrows of the evil one. Take the helmet of salvation and the sword of the Spirit, which is the word of God.

And pray in the Spirit on all occasions with all kinds of prayers and requests. With this in mind, be alert and always keep on praying for all the Lord's people. Pray also for me, that whenever I speak, words may be given me so that I will fearlessly make known the mystery of the gospel, for which I am an ambassador in chains. Pray that I may declare it fearlessly, as I should.

How well prepared are you to fulfill the mission God has given you?

What are you willing to do so that you are not ill-prepared for the mission and are not surprised by the suddenness or intensity of Satan's attacks?

Study Two | Roman "Justice" Comes Quickly

The Very Words of God

After they had been severely flogged, they were thrown into prison, and the jailer was commanded to guard them carefully. When he received these orders, he put them in the inner cell and fastened their feet in the stocks.

Acts 16:23–24

Bible Discovery

A Night in Prison

Judgment on the charges brought against Paul and Silas came swiftly and without mercy. Unless the accused was a Roman citizen, the magistrates of a colony could enforce the law related to the slave owners' complaints without further legal proceeding. So Paul and Silas received the usual punishment for causing a public disturbance: flogging.

The severity of a flogging varied by the instruments the *lictors* (the officers of the magistrates who carried out such punishments) used and the number of blows inflicted. It was not uncommon for a person to die from flogging,[10] and the severe beating Paul and Silas received no doubt left welts and open wounds all over their bodies.[11] Such punishment would not happen to a person known to be a Roman citizen.

In many cases, a brutal flogging was the end of the matter. Whether the accused died or survived didn't matter because Roman justice had been served. But for more serious crimes, flogging preceded additional punishment—perhaps crucifixion, forced gladiatorial combat, or being sold into slavery in the mines or galleys. Apparently, this is what the magistrates had in mind for Paul and Silas because they had them put into prison.

When the order for prison was given, Paul and Silas knew their ordeal was not over. The Romans did not use imprisonment as punishment. Prison was merely a holding place until justice was determined. If Paul and Silas were found innocent, they would be released. If not, they would face punishment far worse than they had experienced already.

Paul and Silas were paying a high price for being faithful to their calling. They were put into the "inner cell" of the prison, the place reserved for foreigners, the worst criminals, and the lower class. It was generally a cave, pit, or subterranean room—a notoriously dark and dirty place. Any food or water that might be available would be unfit to eat or drink. In the filth, with a lack of care for their wounds, many flogged prisoners died.

Even so, Paul did not reveal his Roman citizenship, which would have resulted in immediate release and aid. How would the two men handle the uncertainty and extreme personal risk of their position? What did they anticipate God would do?

1. Paul's commitment to the mission Jesus gave him and his faithfulness in living it out is remarkable. Consider the long list of what he willingly suffered (2 Corinthians 11:23–28) to bring the good news to the Gentiles that Jesus is Savior and Lord. What do you think of his commitment to be a faithful witness of God's kingdom no matter what happened to him?

    What seems to have troubled Paul, perhaps even more than his personal suffering?

    Paul was heroic in his endurance of suffering for the sake of the gospel, but let's not kid ourselves: it was no less painful for him than it would have been for any one of us. How did he feel about what happened to him in Philippi? (See 1 Thessalonians 2:2.)

2. After the *lictors* flogged Paul and Silas, the magistrates remanded the two men to the care of the Philippian jailer, who probably was a former soldier. What special orders did they give regarding how Paul and Silas were to be treated? (See Acts 16:23.)

    The jailer knew he was to guard these prisoners with his very life. What did he do to fulfill his orders and ensure that Paul and Silas could not escape? (See Acts 16:24.)

    What other precaution did the jailer take to prevent their escape, and how would it have added to their suffering that night in their cell? (See Acts 16:26.)

DID YOU KNOW?
To Be in a Roman Prison
A Roman prison was not a place anyone would want to be. In addition to enduring the darkness, filth, and unfit water and food (if there was any), a prisoner also might be locked into stocks or chains.

Roman stocks were heavy wooden planks with holes cut at regular intervals and split lengthwise. One half of the plank was anchored to the floor on edge, and the prisoner's hands and feet were placed into the holes and locked into position by the top plank. Sometimes the prisoner's feet were spread so far apart that the legs were nearly pulled out of joint, causing excruciating pain.[12] The suffering was intense, and sleep was nearly impossible.

In addition, prisoners often were chained with manacles for the wrists and possibly a collar around the neck. This added weight made an already painful situation even more unendurable. Imagine what it would have been like for Paul and Silas, already bruised and bleeding from being flogged, to have the added torment of stocks and chains. Such conditions were reserved for foreigners and slaves, not Roman citizens.

3. Paul and Silas sat in the darkness of an inner cell, likely unable to sleep due to the pain of deep bruises, open wounds, and legs held nearly out of joint. They had received no food or drink. They did not know how much worse their situation might become. In this very dark place, what does Acts 16:25 tell us they did?

Do you think you would have done what they did? Why or why not?

What might you have thought if you had been one of the other prisoners who heard them singing and praising God that night?

4. If we truly are committed to the mission of proclaiming through word and deed the gospel of Jesus Christ, we need to learn more about why and how Paul and Silas did what they did in the Philippian jail.

   a. What were they doing? The Text says they were "praying and singing hymns to God" (Acts 16:25). In Hebrew, *pray* is the verb for *worship*. So in the midst of their pain, misery, and uncertainty, they were worshiping God—singing psalms, reciting Scripture, and praising and praying to God. What kind of commitment does it take to do this under such circumstances?

b. What Scripture might they have been reciting? If Paul followed the custom of other Jews of his day, they might have been reciting the *shema*, the Scripture portion Jesus called the greatest commandment. Jews typically recited it between the setting of the sun and midnight:

> *Hear, O Israel: The Lord our God, the Lord is one. Love the Lord your God with all your heart and with all your soul and with all your strength (Deuteronomy 6:4–5).*

This passage continues with reminders of the importance and prominence of loving God every moment of every day in every part of life:

> *These commandments that I give you today are to be on your hearts. Impress them on your children. Talk about them when you sit at home and when you walk along the road, when you lie down and when you get up. Tie them as symbols on your hands and bind them on your foreheads. Write them on the doorframes of your houses and on your gates (Deuteronomy 6:6–9).*

What impact do you imagine focusing on these words would have had on Paul and Silas, and hearing these words ring out in the night would have on other prisoners and the Roman guards?

c. Why about "midnight"? This question raises interesting possibilities. Paul was a Jewish scholar, a student of the Torah. He was trained to seek to understand every life circumstance and to shape his response in light of God's Word. Whatever happened to him, whatever he did, Paul wanted to be doing what God's Word commanded. So imagine Paul locked in prison, reviewing his memory of God's Word for guidance that fit his situation, and likely remembering these words from one of David's psalms:

> *Though the wicked bind me with ropes, I will not forget your law. At midnight I rise to give you thanks for your righteous laws (Psalm 119:61–62)!*

Paul had been imprisoned by the wicked! He was bound! Do you think he wouldn't praise God for his righteousness at midnight?[13]

If we, as followers of Jesus, want to make an impact on our world, how important is it for us to do all we can to know and live by God's every word?

5. Paul and Silas were God's faithful witnesses every moment of their lives—even when spending those moments in deep darkness and pain in the pit of a Philippian jail. They knew God heard their agony and their prayers. So they continued to put him on display by pouring every bit of strength they had left into worshiping him. What did God "suddenly" do that perhaps even surprised them? (See Acts 16:26.)

DATA FILE
Earthquakes and God's Intervention

When I made my first trip to Philippi, my brilliant guide Kostas Kolizeras, PhD,[14] commented about the earthquake that broke open the Philippian jail where Paul and Silas were held. "Earthquakes are common in this part of Macedonia," he said, "but someone timed this one perfectly!"

Earthquakes are one of several natural metaphors that indicate God's dramatic involvement in the lives of his people. Wind and fire announce his presence and his power. The floods of Noah's day and after Israel's crossing of the Red Sea portray his judgment and anger over human rebellion. Thunder, lightning, and hail announce his presence.

Consider how earthquakes have announced God's appearance at pivotal moments in history:

- David, after God delivered him from Saul, described God's appearance like an earthquake (2 Samuel 22:7–8).

- In Isaiah's prophecy, God's dramatic appearance will come with thunder, noise, a devouring fire, a windstorm, a tempest, and an earthquake (Isaiah 29:6).

- Upon Jesus' death on the cross, an earthquake tore the veil of the temple and opened tombs (Matthew 27:45–54). The earthquake added an apocalyptic or history-changing dimension to what God was doing in his redemptive story.

- After the disciples were released from prison and met with followers of Jesus for prayer, the room where they met was shaken as a sign of God's affirmation and the presence of his Spirit (Acts 4:23–24, 31).

- When God appeared to Israel at Mount Sinai, the earth shook at the sound of his voice. It will happen again when Jesus returns to earth (Hebrews 12:18–28).

- The earthquake at the Philippian jail not only released Paul and Silas from their chains but was a dramatic sign of his presence with them (Acts 16:26).

Reflection

Paul and Silas had been beaten severely. Their wounds were not cleaned or bandaged. They were in prison, painfully locked in the stocks with no way to escape or relieve their suffering. Yet they placed their trust entirely in the God of their fathers and worshiped him.

And God heard their cry! He responded to their need in a powerful way—likely far beyond what they hoped. So is this what we should expect God to do when *we* suffer, when we are treated unjustly? The answer is both yes and no.

We know that God hears the cries of those who suffer. He not only hears, he responds—always. But he doesn't necessarily respond in the way we might hope. Sometimes he delivers his people from oppression. Other times he provides just enough strength to endure faithfully. For example, although Paul was released from prison in Philippi, his final imprisonment in Rome ended when he was beheaded by Emperor Nero.

So what is our comfort and where is our courage? Paul and Silas knew that God—however he did it—would provide and empower them to be faithful. In their faithfulness—however they could demonstrate it—they would put God on display and bring glory to his name. It is no different for us.

My father's example stands as a testimony to this. When he learned that he had terminal cancer, he gathered his four sons and asked us to pray for him. I expected him to ask us to pray for healing: a request he wanted but one God did not grant. However, he had a different request. He recited Paul's words from 1 Corinthians 10:31, "So whether you eat or drink or whatever you do, do it all for the glory of God." Then he said, "Please pray that whether I am cured of cancer or die from it that I bring glory to God."

That is how God's people are to seek his provision and deliverance whether they face persecution for their faith, hardship in pursuit of the mission, or suffering in the face of death. Our task of bringing glory, honor, and praise to God never changes.

When life is good and everything is as it should be, how much of a priority is it for you to bring glory, honor, and praise to God? And how do you do it?

When life is hard, when you are suffering, if you are oppressed for your faith, how do you keep your focus on bringing glory, honor, and praise to God?

Study Three | The Philippian Jailer Is Set Free

The Very Words of God

> You have heard that it was said, "Love your neighbor and hate your enemy." But I tell you, love your enemies and pray for those who persecute you, that you may be children of your Father in heaven.
>
> *Matthew 5:43–45*

Bible Discovery

The Jailer Joins the Mission

As Paul and Silas worshiped in the filth and darkness of the Philippian jail, God showed up. And he didn't show up quietly. He made his presence known in a big way—through a powerful earthquake that literally broke open the doors of the jail and set prisoners free from their chains! Not only did God wreak havoc in Philippi's jail, he was unleashing a new chapter in the expansion of his kingdom there.

Paul and Silas, of course, interpreted the earthquake as God's handiwork, his intervention in their suffering. God had set them free so they could have escaped, yet they (and the other prisoners!) did not. They stayed in place, and Luke turns our attention to another key player in this story: the Philippian jailer.

The jailer likely was a hardened soldier who had seen and participated in great violence and cruelty to bring about *Pax Romana* (Roman peace) and enforce Roman justice. But the late-night earthquake shook every dimension of his life to the core. Paul and Silas knew that the earthquake was God's work, but the pagan people of the Roman Empire believed that earthquakes were the work of their gods or a sign of their presence.[15] So to the jailer's way of thinking, some deity was very angry and responsible for shaking the earth and destroying the jail. That was unsettling. But on a personal level, the jailer was terrified. He was personally responsible for every prisoner, and if any escaped, he knew that he would likely pay the price with his life, and his family could suffer great harm as well. Let's see how the dust settled in Philippi.

1. The earthquake jolted the jailer awake. Seeing the prison doors open, he naturally assumed the prisoners had escaped. Faced with that situation, what did the terrified jailer intend to do? (See Acts 16:27.)

   Motivated by compassion and willing to risk his own life for a man who had contributed to his unjust treatment, what amazing news did Paul shout out to the jailer? (See Acts 16:28.)

After the jailer investigated the situation in the "opened" prison, how did he approach Paul and Silas, and what did he want to know? (See Acts 16:29–30.)

DID YOU KNOW?
An Honorable Suicide

In the Roman criminal justice system, magistrates and prison officials were fully responsible for the prisoners in their charge. The escape of even one prisoner could result in unthinkable consequences for the officials involved. They would be publicly shamed and punished—perhaps brutally flogged or executed—according to their level of negligence and the severity of the prisoner's crime. There was no excuse, mercy, or recourse from the courts, the official's superiors, or any deities.

In the case of the Philippian jailer, the magistrates' order was clear: guard them carefully. If Paul and Silas had escaped, the jailer had failed in his duty and was in serious trouble. For a soldier who likely took great pride in his honor, the dishonor of public flogging or execution would have been more than he could bear. Furthermore, if he were to be executed, his estate probably would go to the state rather than to his family, leaving them to be sold into slavery.[16]

Faced with these possibilities within the rigid confines of Roman-style justice and culture, it is likely that the jailer decided his only honorable option was to commit suicide. He then would be viewed as more honorable in the community, and his estate would pass to his family.[17] Evidently, he was a man of honor who loved his family enough to die in order to save them from a dreadful future. Ironically, God had an even more honorable plan for him—a gift that Jesus, God's Son, purchased with the price of his own life.

2. From ancient times to the present day, God has given his people the mission to live in a way that brings glory to his name and makes him known to those who do not yet know him. It is amazing to see this happening as the story of the Philippian jailer unfolds. The courage and commitment of Paul and Silas to stay in jail rather than escape, and by doing so to show greater care for their jailer's life than for their own, was as powerful an "act of God" in the jailer's eyes as the earthquake. Their example presented God's character and love so clearly that the jailer fell at their feet. With great respect, he asked, "Sirs, what must I do to be saved?" (Acts 16:30).

   We need to be careful to not view his question through our theological understanding. The jailer was a pagan who had no knowledge of God's plan of redemption or a promised Messiah, no concept of sin or the need for forgiveness in order to receive God's gift of eternal life. When he asked this question, he may have been asking how he could be spared from judgment by their God who had sent the earthquake because of how he had treated them, or how he might escape punishment by the Roman authorities because his prisoners were no longer secure. Whatever his understanding, he needed to be informed of the gospel of Jesus Christ.

   a. How did Paul and Silas explain the gospel? (See Acts 16:31–32.)

b. Paul's simple answer is the central invitation of the kingdom of heaven. How is his answer like that of John's explanation for why he wrote his gospel and what Peter proclaimed on Pentecost? (See John 20:30–31; Acts 2:37–39.)

c. How would you state that simple, but profound, invitation?

3. In Roman culture, those who were important and valued were served by others; the Romans did not humble themselves to serve others.

a. In contrast to the Roman way, what are the hallmarks of a true follower of Jesus? (See Matthew 20:26–28; Luke 22:24–27; 1 Peter 4:10.)

b. What remarkable things did the jailer do for Paul and Silas that demonstrated his change of heart—that he had been set free from bondage to the kingdom of this world and its ways—and proved the authenticity of his choice to follow Jesus and join the mission of extending the reign of the one true God in Philippi? (See Acts 16:33–34.)

4. What a night it had been for Paul and Silas, the other prisoners, the guards, and the jailer and his household. And it wasn't yet over! What surprising news did Paul and Silas receive at daybreak, and what was Paul's even more surprising response? (See Acts 16:35–39.)

When Paul and Silas announced their Roman citizenship and listed the unlawful treatment that had violated their rights, it sent shock waves through the Roman officials of Philippi. Suddenly the tables had turned. Paul held the power over the magistrates because they faced the possibility of penalties for mistreating Roman citizens that were as severe as the injustices Paul and Silas had suffered: flogging and possible execution. What did Paul demand the magistrates do, and what attitude did they demonstrate when approaching him?

When Paul and Silas demanded that the magistrates come to them and publicly "escort" them from the rubble that had been the prison, what do you think Paul was forcing them to recognize?

THINK ABOUT IT
Paul Uses His Roman Citizenship to Advance God's Kingdom

The way Paul used his Roman citizenship in Philippi was not typical for a Roman. Most Romans were proud of their status and used its rights and privileges to their full advantage. But Paul's citizenship in God's kingdom was far more important to him than being a Roman. He preferred to be known as a Jew who followed Jesus as his Savior and Lord. He rarely played his "citizenship card" unless doing so would make the gospel message known and advance the cause of God's kingdom.

As one writer observed, "Paul's sense of identity came first from his Christian faith, secondly from his Jewish heritage, and only thirdly from his Greco-Roman heritage."[18]

It seems that Paul knew his Roman citizenship would give him influence over the political brokers of Philippi. He may have realized that the small community of believers he would leave behind in Philippi faced great risks as they lived out their loyalty to Jesus as Savior and Lord in a Roman colony. By revealing his citizenship long after it could be of any help to him, he put the magistrates in a vulnerable position. They were relieved to appease him in any way they could, and by publicly releasing Paul and Silas, they demonstrated that their message and the way they lived it out did not violate Roman law after all. So I believe Paul waited for the right time and used his citizenship to provide "cover" for the new believers to practice their faith.

5. After they were released, and before they moved on to where God would lead them next, what did Paul and Silas do? (See Acts 16:40.)

As you think about that small gathering of new believers in Philippi, what do you think may have encouraged Lydia and the jailer and their households and others, who were not identified?

What about their experiences in Philippi do you think may have encouraged Paul and Silas?

Reflection

When Paul went to Philippi, he had a mission to bring the gospel message: that the kingdom of heaven, the kingdom of Messiah Jesus had come. He would display that message by showing through his own actions what life looks like when Jesus is Savior and Lord. It would not be easy to establish a colony of heaven in the midst of the Roman colony of Philippi. The values and lifestyle of the kingdom Paul represented opposed those of Rome, and its master, Satan. That kingdom would defend its turf fiercely.

As the kingdom of heaven and the kingdom of this world clashed, Paul found himself squarely in the cross fire. Physically he paid a high price as Satan's kingdom assaulted him with false accusations, injustices, and brutal punishment. But even when the opportunity to escape presented itself, Paul chose to continue the mission, trusting in God to provide and lead the way. By doing so, he had the opportunity to reach out in love to the Philippian jailer who was partly responsible for the painful, unjust abuse he suffered. Paul not only helped to save the jailer's life, he led him to believe and inherit eternal life! The man went from being dead to living forever. He went from carrying out the orders of Rome to modeling the love of Jesus.

Imagine Paul's excitement as he saw the jailer's commitment to follow and serve Jesus. It might seem that the jailer would be one of the least likely people in Philippi to join the kingdom of heaven. But through the baptism of his household, the jailer joyfully made the public declaration that the Lord, the God of the Jews, was the God he served.

> Who in your world seems like one of the least likely people to be set free from bondage to the kingdom of this world and to be restored to the kingdom of heaven?

> To what extent and in which specific ways does your life— not just what you say, but what you do—lead that person to ask, "What can I do to be saved?"

What is your commitment to pray for that person, to faithfully display God's love and character, and ask him to "show up" in the occasional earthquake when you have done all that you can do?

CONFRONTING THE EMPIRE

At Mount Sinai, God commissioned the Hebrew people to be his partners in advancing his great plan of redemption by making him known to the Gentile world. As part of his plan to continue gathering Gentiles into the kingdom of heaven, God chose and commissioned Paul to be his herald of the good news that the long-awaited Messiah had come. Paul eagerly accepted this mission and traveled throughout the Roman world preaching the gospel of Jesus and demonstrating God's love to both Jew and Gentile. Everywhere he went—Jerusalem, Damascus, Ephesus, Athens, Rome, or the far reaches of the Roman Empire—he proclaimed Jesus as God's anointed, the Savior and Lord of the world that the ancient Hebrew Text said he would be.

Paul's teaching was clear: the redemptive work of Messiah Jesus opened the door for all people, calling them to reject the false gods of the kingdom of this world, submit to his reign, and experience "the obedience that comes from faith."[1] He instructed all those who believed to live holy lives that would affirm the gospel and bear fruit in the hearts of a watching world.[2] His goal was not simply to provide a different religious experience, but to present Jesus—the Jewish Messiah—as the one true Savior, Lord, and King who dispelled chaos and brought the peace of the kingdom of heaven—*shalom*—to all who followed him.

Try to imagine Paul's excitement as he left Philippi. He was leaving behind a community of Jews and Gentiles joined together as one family of Jesus followers. Already they had demonstrated their commitment to live in a way that displayed the *shalom* of God's kingdom in that Roman colony. As he walked west on the

Via Egnatia, we can almost hear the thoughts he would later write:

> *Consequently, you are no longer foreigners and strangers, but fellow citizens with God's people and also members of his household, built on the foundation of the apostles and prophets, with Christ Jesus himself as the chief cornerstone. In him the whole building is joined together and rises to become a holy temple in the Lord. And in him you too are being built together to become a dwelling in which God lives by his Spirit.[3]*

As Paul explained the gospel message in cities large and small, he often saw the kingdom of heaven come in power and bring peace to individuals and entire communities. But as Paul traveled closer to Rome, he increasingly encountered a world of chaos where a different "lord" and "savior" reigned. So the good news of the *shalom* of God's kingdom that Paul proclaimed consistently ran into opposition from the idolatry, immorality, injustice, and oppression that the gospel of Caesar called peace.

Ahead of Paul was Thessalonica, a city with a long history of experiencing conflict between kingdoms. As a port city poised between the Aegean Sea and the *Via Egnatia*, Thessalonica often was in the path of conflicting kingdoms seeking expansion to the east as well as to the west. It was the launching point for Alexander the Great's Hellenistic conquest of territory all the way to Egypt and India. But as the Macedonian kingdom waned, the Thessalonians faced increasing conflict with the Roman Empire expanding from the west. Eventually the city fell to Rome and, like the rest of Macedonia, was ransacked and nearly destroyed.

Nearly a century later, when the conflict between Marc Antony and Octavian (Caesar Augustus)—who favored an empire—and Cassius and Brutus—who favored a republic—erupted in battle on the Plain of Drama outside Philippi, Thessalonica once again had to choose which kingdom it would serve. They chose Marc Antony and Octavian, and when the alliance between the two victors led to war once again, the Thessalonians chose Octavian. When he became Emperor Augustus, Octavian generously expressed his gratitude for the Thessalonians' loyalty, providing funds for capital improvements and the amenities that defined

Roman "peace." The Thessalonians gladly submitted to the authority of Rome, even worshiping Caesar as the divine son of a god in exchange for peace, security, and prosperity.

So when Paul came to Thessalonica, the people had significant reasons to ensure that nothing would diminish the gospel of divine Caesar or threaten the peace he bestowed. Would God raise up a "temple," a dwelling place for the Holy Spirit in the hearts and lives of his people, in that city too? Or would the kingdom already established there resist the kingdom of heaven that Paul proclaimed?

Opening Thoughts (3 minutes)

The Very Words of God

> As was his custom, Paul went into the synagogue, and on three Sabbath days he reasoned with them from the Scriptures, explaining and proving that the Messiah had to suffer and rise from the dead. "This Jesus I am proclaiming to you is the Messiah," he said.
>
> **Acts 17:2–3**

Think About It

As individuals and as a society, culture, and nation, we experience pivotal events in our lives and collective history. How we experience these events become defining moments that shape and influence not only our lives but may impact generations to come. For Americans, some of these events might be the Civil War, the Trail of Tears, the Great Depression, the Holocaust, Pearl Harbor, or 9-11.

In what ways do you see that these, or other defining moments, affect our cultural consciousness, societal behavior, or personal response to situations we encounter today?

Which historical events might have affected the Thessalonians' response to the gospel message brought by Paul in about 50 AD? Any ideas?

Video Notes (33 minutes)

Alexander the Great: a legacy of conquest for Hellenism

Paul: ambassador of a very different kingdom

Thessalonica and the kingdom of this world at the time of Paul

Benefactions: great rewards in return for loyalty

"Good works" to honor Rome and its deified emperors

Advancing the worship of Caesar

The language of worship

Paul comes to Thessalonica and reasons from the Scriptures

The kingdoms of Jesus and Caesar collide

A city in turmoil

Are we armed to bring the gospel of Christ's kingdom to our world?

Video Discussion (7 minutes)

1. In the Roman world, where people knew the price of being on the wrong side of *Pax Romana* and where about one-third of the people were slaves, how important was it to court the favor of the Roman emperor?

    On the map on page 207, note the strategic location of Thessalonica, the first major city on the *Via Egnatia* east of Rome and on the route to Asia Minor. What risks might the people of Thessalonica face if the city fell out of Caesar's favor?

How high a price might you have been willing to pay for Caesar's benefactions?

2. Based on the video presentation, what did you discover about the role of conflict and conquest in the ancient world and the impact it had on ordinary people in the course of everyday life?

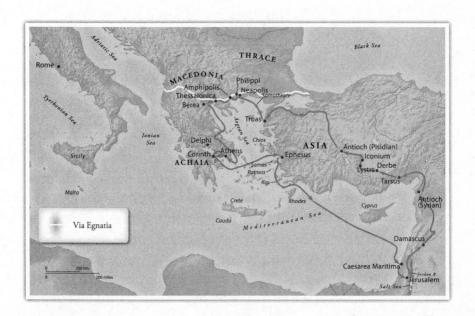

What have you realized about the delicate position Paul
was in for bringing an opposing gospel—the gospel of
Jesus Christ, the true Savior, Lord, and King—to Thessalonica?

3. What surprised you about the customary language of worship used in reference to the deified Roman emperors?

In what ways do you think such language helped or
hindered the sharing of the gospel message? Explain your
answer.

What do people hear and think when we say "gospel," or
"good news," and to what extent do they respond to it as
we expect they would?

Small Group Bible Discovery and Discussion (12 minutes)

Paul "Reasoned" with Them from the Scriptures

Paul was born about the same time as Jesus into a family that was faithful to know and obey the Torah. While growing up, Paul also was a devoted and brilliant student of the Torah. He excelled in both knowledge and interpretation of the Hebrew Bible and studied in Jerusalem under Rabbi Gamaliel, a highly respected expert on the Torah whose interpretations were often similar to those of Jesus.

Known as the greatest of all Jewish sages, Gamaliel certainly influenced Paul's teaching. As a disciple of Gamaliel, Paul was trained to apply the Torah to the Hellenistic worldview of Roman culture, a skill he used extensively in his role as the "rabbi to the Gentiles." Paul also followed Gamaliel's practice of writing epistles.

However, prior to meeting Jesus on the road to Damascus, Paul chose a path quite different from that which Gamaliel taught. Paul was intensely passionate about the Torah, as we might expect, and zealously opposed those who interpreted it differently from what he believed. In Paul's time, zeal (*qana* in Hebrew) was understood to mean strong—even violent—action taken against those who compromised with the Gentiles and their ways, thus turning away God's anger from his people. This led to his persecution of the followers of Jesus in an effort to destroy the early church,[4] an action that Gamaliel did not support. In fact, Gamaliel stated to the Sanhedrin that followers of Jesus should be left alone because if their teaching was not from God, it would soon pass away; and if it was from God, the Jews who opposed it would be fighting against God.[5]

Then, in a turn of events Paul never imagined, he met Jesus and learned that he was God's chosen instrument to make the name and redeeming work of Jesus known to the Gentiles! Knowing the Text as he did, Paul realized that the commission Jesus gave him to take the gospel to the Gentiles was a continuation of God's commission to Israel and the prophets. No wonder we see in Paul such an intense commitment to take the good news of God's kingdom to the ends of the earth. He can barely contain the privilege of being God's light to the nations so that the Gentiles might glorify God for his mercy: "Therefore I will praise you among the Gentiles; I will sing the praises of your name. . . . Rejoice, you Gentiles, with his people!"[6]

1. Where, according to Acts 17:1–4, did Paul and his companions go when they arrived in Thessalonica, and why?

Why was it important for Paul, a superb scholar of the Hebrew Bible, to know the Scriptures as well as he did in order to accomplish his mission in Thessalonica, and how effective was he as a result?

Where had Paul done this before, and what impact did he have on those who heard him? (See Acts 9:19–22; 13:2–5, 13–16, 32–44.)

DID YOU KNOW?
God Prepared a People and a Place for the Gospel Message

God prepared the Roman Empire in many ways to receive the good news of the Messiah's coming. Some of these preparations had been in place for centuries. Consider, for example, the presence of Jewish communities in nearly every major city of the empire. Some of these communities were established between 740–722 BC as a result of the dispersion of captives by the Assyrians following their conquest of the Northern Kingdom of Israel. Other communities resulted from Babylon's conquest of Judah in 587–586 BC. Still other communities were established by refugees from these conflicts and by Jewish merchants who traded with cities throughout the Mediterranean world.

These communities of Jews became known for their devotion to the Text and righteous living in obedience to God's laws. The Jewish faith was a legal religion in the Roman Empire, which allowed synagogues to exist for worship. The synagogues ensured a biblically literate audience that would understand the message of the long-awaited Messiah. In addition, early followers of Jesus were viewed as being a part of the Jewish community and synagogue and therefore received the coverage of legal status in the Roman Empire. Indeed, the Jewish synagogues provided a fertile environment for the good news of Jesus to take root and flourish.

2. The response of a "large number" of God-fearing Gentiles to Paul's "reasoning from the Scriptures" apparently upset the status quo in the synagogue of Thessalonica.

   a. What was the source of the problem, and what trouble ensued? (See Acts 17:5–9.)

b. Which accusation threw the entire city into turmoil, and why would this have created a major problem in Thessalonica? (See Acts 17:7.)

3. After the violent turn of events in Thessalonica, what was Paul's next move? (See Acts 17:10–12.)

What does this reveal about his commitment to the mission God gave him?

What was different about the way the gospel message was received in that city, and what impact do you think this had on Paul and the advancement of God's kingdom?

4. Paul's methodology for presenting the good news of the Messiah was to "reason" (*dielexato*) with people from the Scriptures. This means he did not "preach" the gospel message but instead followed the rabbinic practice of dialogue with his audience. He would use various texts from the Hebrew Bible to present and support his interpreta-

tions, which his audience would then evaluate according to their understanding of the Text. For this method to be effective, both speaker and audience had to be significantly familiar with the Text, which would have been the case in Jewish synagogues. Also, by using God's Word as the basis for his message, Paul, in effect, claimed God's promise that the proclamation of his Word will always have the exact effect he desires: "It will not return to me empty, but will accomplish what I desire and achieve the purpose for which I sent it" (Isaiah 55:10–11).

a. Which strategy did Paul continue to use to make the gospel message known in Athens, Corinth, and Ephesus, and what responses did he receive? (See Acts 17:13–23; 18:1–8, 18–19; 19:8–10.)

b. Who else did Paul reason with when those who worshiped in the synagogue rejected the gospel message? How had he learned to do this, and how effective was his strategy?

Faith Lesson (4 minutes)

At Mount Sinai, God gave his chosen people the mission to make him known among the nations. He established his people in the Promised Land where they were to demonstrate what life looked like when he was in control. At times God's people were faithful to their mission, but often they followed a different path and served a different master—engaging in immorality, serving themselves while oppressing the poor, practicing injustice, and worshiping other gods. Eventually, God removed them from the Promised Land. He allowed the beloved temple to be destroyed and his people to be exiled to Babylon far away from the land they had called home.

During that time Jeremiah, the great prophet of God, wrote in a letter to the devastated exiles:

> *This is what the Lord Almighty, the God of Israel, says to all those I carried into exile from Jerusalem to Babylon: "Build houses and settle down; plant gardens and eat what they produce. Marry and have sons and daughters; find wives for your sons and give your daughters in marriage, so that they too may have sons and daughters. Increase in number there; do not decrease. Also, seek the peace and prosperity of the city to which I have carried you into exile. Pray to the Lord for it, because if it prospers, you too will prosper" (Jeremiah 29:4–7).*

Even while enslaved, God's people were still called to fulfill the mission! God instructed this tiny, enslaved minority who had no status or power in their world to remain faithful to God's commands and to be fruitful and multiply. And they did. As a minority, they lived out their faith in such a way that others—even kings who ruled over them—were drawn to the God of Israel.[7]

In Paul's day, Jewish people in the Roman Empire faced a similar situation. They were a distinct minority, at best perhaps 10 percent of the population. Despite hardship and persecution, they sought to live in faithful obedience to God and promote the well-being of the culture in which they lived. Large numbers of Gentiles were attracted to the living example of *shalom* they witnessed within the Jewish communities and chose to serve their God. Then Paul (and others) showed up with the gospel message, the good news that Messiah—the true Savior and Lord— had come! Not only did many Jews accept this news because it was true to the Text, but many Gentiles who had joined their communities believed as well.

But the climate for the new community of Jesus followers was risky. They lived under the shadow of Caesar's imperial cult, and nowhere was this more pervasive than in Thessalonica. The worship of Caesar in Thessalonica was a significant gesture of gratitude for the benefits and special relationship the city enjoyed with Rome. Any threat to this mutually beneficial relationship—even something as simple as the statement of the truth of the gospel of Christ or the testimony of a righteous life—would generate a strong reaction.

1. If we are going to be living witnesses of the truth of the gospel of Christ—representatives of God's kingdom—we must realize that we will be in conflict with the kingdom of the world that surrounds us. That, however, does not change the mission to which God has called us. If you are living a life that puts God on display, in what specific ways might you be considered a threat to the community or culture in which you live?

    What can (and will) you do to make the most of this opportunity—not to win an argument or to show yourself to be "better" than someone else but to better explain or demonstrate the gospel message?

2. In many places today, the community of Jesus followers is losing status and influence within the dominant culture. How does this make it more difficult to fulfill the mission God has given you?

Conversely, how does this truth create more opportunities or make it easier?

Closing (1 minute)

Read 1 Peter 3:13–16 aloud together: "Who is going to harm you if you are eager to do good? But even if you should suffer for what is right, you are blessed. 'Do not fear their threats; do not be frightened.' But in your hearts revere Christ as Lord. Always be prepared to give an answer to everyone who asks you to give the reason for the hope that you have. But do this with gentleness and respect, keeping a clear conscience, so that those who speak maliciously against your good behavior in Christ may be ashamed of their slander."

Then pray, thanking God for his faithfulness in redeeming us, his rebellious creation. Praise him for his graciousness in making us his partners in advancing his great plan of redemption. Ask for his guidance and help in making us willing disciples who will learn and obey his ways so that we too may be effective in making the gospel of Christ known. Pray for a heart of humility and love that displays God's character in every encounter we have. May God's kingdom come and reign in our world!

Memorize

Who is going to harm you if you are eager to do good? But even if you should suffer for what is right, you are blessed. "Do not fear their threats; do not be frightened." But in your hearts revere Christ as Lord. Always be prepared to give an answer to everyone who asks you to give the reason for the hope that you have. But do this with gentleness and respect, keeping a clear conscience, so that those who speak maliciously against your good behavior in Christ may be ashamed of their slander.

1 Peter 3:13–16

The Gospel of Christ Provokes Imperial Rome

In-Depth Personal Study Sessions

Study One | Paul: Prepared for Confrontation

The Very Words of God

> *"These men who have caused trouble all over the world have now come here. . . . They are all defying Caesar's decrees, saying that there is another king, one called Jesus." When they heard this, the crowd and the city officials were thrown into turmoil.*

Acts 17:6–8

Bible Discovery

Thessalonica Clings to the Gospel of Caesar

Paul arrived in Thessalonica in 50 AD during the reign of Claudius, the Roman emperor who ousted Jews from the city of Rome.[8] So even before Paul brought the news of another gospel, another king, and another kingdom to the province of Macedonia, there existed in the Roman Empire an underlying tension or suspicion related to any kind of unrest the Jewish community might stir up. And in Thessalonica, the tension was heightened.

The citizens of Thessalonica were proud of their historic roots. Alexander the Great had come from their region, and their city became the staging area for his campaign to extend the Macedonian kingdom as far east as India and as far south as Egypt. They took pride in the fame and glory of his conquests and how his efforts to spread Hellenism—the Greek ideals and lifestyle—had shaped the culture of the ancient world. Although the advance of Alexander's kingdom ended with his death in 323 BC, the city still carried reminders of its Hellenistic past. The majority of inscriptions found in the city's ruins are written in Greek rather than Latin. And, although the Romans defeated the Macedonian kingdom in 168 BC, Hellenistic culture lived on in the Roman civilization.

The citizens of Thessalonica were also proud of—and prospered greatly from—the relationship they had cultivated with Rome. They had supported Octavian, who became Emperor Caesar Augustus, during the war to avenge the assassination of his father, Julius Caesar, in 42 BC. They supported Octavian again during his final battle against Marc Antony at Actium in 31 BC. In gratitude, Emperor Augustus recognized Thessalonica as a free city-state, allowing its citizens to govern themselves under the authority of a democratic assembly rather than a Roman governor. He also showered the city with many *benefactions*—known as "blessings" or "good works"—that included refurbishing the seaport and building temples, statues, aqueducts, baths, and a theater.

In the ongoing effort to honor the emperor (and to keep his benefactions flowing in their direction), worship of the emperor became a core element of life in Thessalonica. Its citizens built a temple and established a priesthood for the worship of Julius and Augustus. They minted coins with Julius Caesar, named "God," on one side and Augustus, named "Son of God," on the other. Statues and inscriptions all declared the supreme authority of Rome and "Imperator Caesar, Son of God."

ONE OF THE FINEST STATUES OF CAESAR AUGUSTUS EVER CARVED, THIS PORTRAYAL OF THE EMPEROR IN WHAT IS CALLED THE "DIVINE POSE," CLEARLY PRESENTS HIM AS LORD AND GOD.

When Paul arrived, Thessalonica had enjoyed for more than a century the prosperity, pleasure, and access to power that a loyal Roman city received. Yet the cultural memory of its citizens encompassed both sides of Imperial Rome. They could not forget Rome's ransack and destruction of their city following the Battle of Pydna when the Macedonian kingdom's resistance was finally crushed. All the same, their daily experience of Roman benefactions demonstrated what absolute loyalty to Rome guaranteed. Only their devotion to divine Caesar and everything Roman would keep the benefactions coming their way.

No wonder Paul faced immediate resistance when he brought the good news of Jesus to Thessalonica. From the perspective of its leading officials and authorities, there was simply no way the gospel of Caesar would politely coexist with the gospel of Christ. For Thessalonica, it would be Caesar and Caesar only.

1. The identity of Jesus as the Son of God and his resurrection from the dead are essential truths of the gospel message that Paul and the other apostles taught. Though we don't know exactly which passages Paul used to "reason" (meaning interpret and dialogue) with the worshipers in the synagogue in Thessalonica about Jesus and the promised Messiah, there are a number of options.[9] How, for example, might you "reason" about Isaiah 53 as well as other passages in order to understand the meaning of what Paul taught about the gospel in Pisidian Antioch? (See Isaiah 53; Acts 13:26–41.)

2. The implications of the Christian teaching about the resurrection of Jesus frequently aroused conflict in the Roman world. The Jewish community (with the exception of the Sadducees) believed in the idea of bodily resurrection, but it was an unknown concept in the pagan religions of the Greco-Roman world. So, if Jesus actually did rise from the

dead, and his followers will one day rise again too, the world as people understood it was changing. Fundamental change always threatens the world's power structures, and it is particularly threatening to those who benefit from political, social, and financial power. Consider the following examples of how the claim that Jesus had died and risen again "caused trouble all over the world."

a. The Sadducees represented the ruling priesthood in Jerusalem and maintained control and power in cooperation with the Roman authorities. They were wealthy and satisfied with the world system just as it was. How did they respond to the resurrection of Jesus the Messiah? (See Acts 4:1–18; 23:6–10.)

Mary's song in Luke 1:46–55 echoes the prophets' description of God's coming kingdom over which the risen Messiah will reign. What about this coming kingdom could be thought of as "dangerous" and create upheaval for the Sadducees?

b. Nothing in Luke's description of Paul's presentation of the gospel to the Thessalonians indicates that he criticized the Roman emperor or promoted a political agenda. Yet it wasn't difficult for some Jews who were jealous of Paul to cause a riot in the city. What, to the

Philippians' way of thinking, was Paul's offense, and what had he taught that led to that conclusion? (See Acts 17:3, 5–8.)

THINK ABOUT IT
Why Were the Jews Jealous?

When Paul spent time in the synagogue in Thessalonica explaining the gospel message that Jesus was the Messiah, a "large number of God-fearing Greeks and quite a few prominent women" were persuaded to join with Paul and Silas, which made some Jews jealous.[10] Why? Why would some of the Jewish congregation be jealous of Gentiles becoming followers of Jesus?

Part of the answer may be found in the "prominent women" part of Luke's account. The Jewish emphasis on moral living and strong families attracted certain upper-class women to the Jewish community, and some of them apparently supported the synagogue financially. So, Jews who did not accept Paul's interpretation of the Text that Jesus was Messiah may have resented the potential loss of support if these Gentiles favored the community of Jesus followers. Such concerns were not unlike the concerns of Jewish leaders and priests in Jerusalem who feared the potential loss of control and status because of the crowds that followed Jesus.[11]

Also, anti-Semitism was common in the Roman Empire. Although Roman law recognized the right of the Jews to worship their God, they were viewed with a certain amount of suspicion—a strange minority among the pagan cultures in which they lived. Wealthy or important God-fearers within the Jewish worship community provided a buffer, an added degree of political protection for the Jews. If the loyalty of these key Gentiles shifted toward a Judaism centered on Jesus the promised Messiah rather than the synagogue community, it could create a dangerous void that could put some Jewish communities at risk.

c.   When Paul presented his defense before Festus, the
Roman governor of Judea, and Herod Agrippa, the
Jewish king, what point did he make about the testimony of the prophets that received a strong reaction
from Festus and brought an end to their communication? (See Acts 26:19–31.)

What clues do you see in this account that indicate
Festus and Agrippa understood the implications of
Jesus' resurrection?

d.   In Athens, Paul reasoned with the Jews and God-fearing
Gentiles in the synagogue as well as with philosophers
in the public marketplace. What "strange" new idea did
Paul teach that piqued the interest of his Gentile audience, and how did they respond? (See Acts 17:16–20,
31–34.)

3.   Paul had a very impressive résumé for being called to
take the gospel message to the Gentile world. He knew
the Hebrew Bible as well as anyone. We might think he
was 100 percent ready for his mission. In one sense, he
was; he knew the Scriptures. In another sense, he was
not; he needed to reinterpret his understanding of the

Hebrew Text to fit the reality of Jesus and the coming of his kingdom.

Recognizing the identity of Jesus as the Messiah and the coming of the kingdom of heaven through his suffering and redemptive sacrifice—not through the apocalyptic judgment that many Jews expected (and hoped for)—represented a radical change in Paul's thinking. It was also a radical adjustment to not only focus on influencing the Jewish people to faithfully live out the mission God had given to their ancestors at Mount Sinai but to devote himself to bringing the message of God's redemption to the Gentiles.

Paul still served the same God and had the same Bible. He was still part of the same kingdom of priests with the same mission to all nations. He still advanced the reign of the kingdom of heaven. But he needed to retrain and reorient his thinking in order to be prepared to fulfill the mission ahead. Consider how he would do that.[12]

a. Paul was certain of his mission when he headed toward Damascus to find and persecute followers of Jesus. What began to change for Paul when Jesus stopped him on the road to Damascus? (See Acts 9:1–9; 22:3–11.)

b. What new understanding did Ananias share with Paul? (See Acts 9:10–19; 22:12–16.)

c. For how long did Paul "not consult any human being" in the desert environment of Arabia? Why do you think he took this time away, and what might he have wanted to accomplish through it? (See Galatians 1:11–18.)

d. Upon his return from Arabia, who did Paul visit in Jerusalem, and why might Paul have spent time with him? (See Galatians 1:18.) Note: "Cephas" is Peter, who had a leadership role in the community of Jesus followers in Jerusalem.

e. Paul also went to his birthplace in Tarsus of Cilicia where he met Barnabas who, according to tradition not recorded in the Bible, was another follower of Jesus who had been taught by Gamaliel. For a number of years, the two men together taught and discipled followers of Jesus. Even with all he knew, had learned, and had experienced, what did Paul do to ensure he was presenting the gospel the way God intended? (See Galatians 1:21–2:2.)

What do you think of the amount of time, effort, and careful thought Paul put into his preparation to take the gospel to the Gentiles?

DID YOU KNOW?
Paul Didn't Abandon His Jewish Faith

Paul is sometimes viewed as ignoring his "Jewishness" and abandoning his Jewish faith in order to start what would later become the Christian faith. But this was not the case at all. He did not abandon his Jewish faith. He did not renounce his allegiance to the Hebrew Text.

When Paul met Jesus, however, he *did* gain a new understanding of what God's plan of redemption looked like. He discovered that Jesus was the Messiah and that his kingdom would come not by military conquest or divine deliverance but by the living sacrifice of Jesus' followers.

Reflection

It is difficult for us to comprehend what an excellent student of the Hebrew Bible Paul was, and how well prepared he was to present the gospel of Christ to both Jews and Gentiles. As followers of Jesus today, we too must be prepared. Above all, we must become better students of the Bible if we want to share the good news of God's kingdom and make an impact on our culture. The inspired Word of God, anointed by his Spirit, was the basis for Paul's discussions with people—both Jews and Gentiles—of his world. The power of God's Word authenticated his message and opened the hearts and minds of those who heard him.

It's no different for us. Yes, our lifestyle (if we truly live in a way that puts God on display and advances his kingdom) is essential, because the *shalom* of God's kingdom attracts people who do not know him. A good example is the Gentile woman, Ruth, who saw the faith and lives of her mother- and father-in-law and decided to join the community of God's people.[13] But we must not overlook the Word of God. Our knowledge and application of God's Word is what plants the seed of God's truth in the human heart where it can grow and bear fruit in a life of faith.

No matter how vehemently Satan's kingdom opposes us, no matter how insignificant and outcast a minority we may be in our culture, God's Word is anointed. When it goes out, it will always accomplish the exact purpose he intends. So if we have open minds and hearts to fulfill God's mission for us, if we are to influence those who are drawn to us because of how we live, then we must be students of the Text!

So how prepared are you to take the gospel of Jesus to your world and extend the reign of God's kingdom?

As you read about how God prepared Paul for the mission, what did you realize about your preparedness?

In Ephesians 6:10–17, Paul uses the language of warfare—not to suggest violent, physical battle to conquer the world for God— but to urge followers of Jesus to be fully prepared to extend God's kingdom in the world. Our battle is not against "flesh and blood" but against the evil one. We do not fight as the world fights, but we are not lightly armed!

Prayerfully consider the armor Paul urges followers of Jesus to use in the battle for God's kingdom and how each applies to your preparation:

The belt of truth

The breastplate of righteousness

The "sandals" of readiness

The shield of faith

The helmet of salvation

The sword of the Spirit

Study Two | The Language of Two Gospels

The Very Words of God

The beginning of the good news about Jesus the Messiah, the Son of God.

Mark 1:1

Bible Discovery

A Conflict Conducted in Words

Paul never viewed his calling to be an ambassador of the gospel of Jesus Christ as a political mission. He never sought to conquer earthly kingdoms, depose rulers, or claim the property of others as his own. His mission was to bring the gospel to the Gentiles and present Jesus as Messiah in exactly the way the Hebrew Bible and Jesus himself described. But there is more to the story.

The reaction of the Roman world to the gospel of Christ is the other half. For Rome, the good news of Jesus that Paul brought was not viewed as merely a threat but an all-out attack. The implications of Paul's message clearly undermined the truth claims of Imperial Rome. If Jesus is Lord of all, then Caesar is not. If Jesus is Savior of the world, then Caesar is not. If Jesus is the Son of God, Caesar must not be. Of course, such a message caused significant consternation in Thessalonica.

To be clear, Paul and Silas weren't accused of saying, "Caesar isn't king," but they were accused of saying, "Jesus is King." That, by implication, did not violate Roman law but violated Caesar's imperial decrees,[14] which was a serious offense. At the time, the imperial cult—the worship of Caesar as divine—was growing rapidly. Emperors claimed the title "son of god" based on the deification of their deceased predecessors. Given the prosperity and security—the *Pax Romana*—Caesar had brought to the empire, people willingly worshiped him.

When Paul and Silas arrived in Thessalonica, everyone knew the good news, but it wasn't the good news of Christ; it was the good news of Caesar. The Thessalonians believed a gospel message that presented Caesar as the son of god, lord of the world. Caesar claimed allegiance from all people of the earth[15] for bringing "salvation," the peace of deliverance from war and poverty, to the entire world. Opposition to this "gospel" of Caesar was dealt with brutally, sometimes by crucifixion.

When Paul "reasoned with them from the Scriptures" to explain what the coming of Jesus the Messiah meant, the Thessalonians heard his message differently from the way we might understand it. Paul naturally used some of the same terms to speak of the gospel of Christ that Rome used in reference to Caesar, so his audience would have recognized immediately the significant implications of his message and its inherent opposition to Imperial Rome. His audience would have heard two kingdoms making strong claims that could not be true for both. Let's consider the impact of Paul's use of "gospel" language on an audience with strong loyalty to the Roman Empire and to their benefactor, the emperor.

1. Many Christians today assume that *evangelion*, translated "gospel" or "good news," is primarily a religious word that applies specifically to Jesus and his gift of eternal life for all who believe. But the word has a broader historical meaning. It was used in ancient Hebrew and Greek to refer generally to the good news brought by a messenger. For people of the Roman Empire, the term specifically referred to good news about an emperor—his coronation, great accomplishment, or the birth of an heir.

   a. What is the "good news" of what God has done, and will do, that the prophet describes in Isaiah 40:9–11 and 52:7–10?

   b. What implications of the "good news" of Jesus' coming—even as king of a kingdom that is "not of this world"—could be perceived as a violation of Caesar's decrees? (See Mark 1:1–2; Luke 2:10–11; John 18:33–37; 19:7–16.)

Why would a loyal Roman citizen living in Thessalonica during the first century be inclined to protest and riot if someone came to town and announced the arrival of a new ruler—a new King, Son of God, and Lord of all?

THINK ABOUT IT
The Gospel of Augustus

In the ancient city of Priene, a calendar inscription from 9 BC reads:

> Since Providence, which has ordered all things and is deeply interested in our life, has set in most perfect order by giving us Augustus, whom she filled with virtue that he might benefit humankind, sending him as a savior, both for us and for our descendants, that he might end war and arrange all things, and since he, Caesar, by his appearance (excelled even our anticipations), surpassing all previous benefactors, and not even leaving to posterity any hope of surpassing what he has done, and since the birthday of the god Augustus was the beginning of the good news [gospel] for the world that came by reason of him which Asia resolved in Smyrna.[16]

So when Mark begins his gospel with the words, "The beginning of the good news about Jesus the Messiah, the Son of God," we can see that there would be conflict with an emperor, his empire, and his people who believed "the birthday of the god Augustus was the beginning of the good news for the world." How would the Roman world deal with two gospels, two kingdoms, and two kings? How would the gospel of the God who reigns, who brings peace, and who proclaims salvation be received by people who already had a gospel of an emperor who demanded absolute loyalty, recognition, honor, and worship?

2. The title Son of God was used to identify Jesus, but it also was used to identify the Roman emperor, especially on coins and inscriptions.

    a. In the following passages, who used the title Son of God to identify Jesus? Why is it significant that each of these parties identified him this way?

The Text	Who identifies Jesus as Son of God?	Why is this designation significant?
Matthew 4:1–6		
Matthew 8:29; Luke 4:40–41		
Matthew 14:33; 16:13–16; John 20:31		
Mark 1:9–11; 9:2–7		
Luke 1:30–35		
Luke 22:66–71		
Acts 9:20–22; Romans 1:1–5, 9		
Mark 15:37–39		

    b. Obviously the "Son of God" title for Jesus could not be ignored or overlooked. It was foundational to the identity of Jesus because, in him, God had come as Savior and King. Furthermore, the title was a direct affront to the gospel of Rome. Imperial inscriptions written in Greek gave the emperor the title "Son of God" (*uios theos*), which is the same title Mark used in his gospel, believed to have been written to believers in Rome: "The beginning of the good news [gospel] about Jesus the Messiah, the Son of God (*uiou theou*)." What do you think any Jew, Gentile, God-fearer, or pagan in the Roman Empire would hear in that statement—about the Roman emperor? About Jesus?

DID YOU KNOW?
The Roman "Son of God"

The title "Son of God," in reference to the Roman emperor, often appeared on coins and inscriptions. For example, a tribute coin from the reign of Tiberius reads, "The worshiped son of a worshiped god." It is important to note that the Latin term is *divi filius,* meaning the son of a deified one, not *deus*, which refers exclusively to gods such as Jupiter or Mars who were considered eternally divine. So the divine claim of the Roman emperors referred to the granting of deification after death, not a statement that they were actually gods. The Greek language did not make such a distinction, so the same term was used to declare the deity of both the emperor and Jesus.

3. To the Roman way of thinking, Caesar, the son of god, came to save the people of the Roman Empire. He saved them from war by bringing victory and peace. He saved them from danger by eliminating bandits and pirates. He saved them from financial and cultural poverty by providing economic prosperity, running water, paved roads, and the amusements of the theater, festivals, and games. All he accomplished showed how Caesar, the "savior," made Rome great again.

a. Although the proclamation of the gospel that Jesus is Savior was not political in any way, what did it suggest about Caesar's "qualifications" and "accomplishments" as savior? (See Luke 2:8–11; Acts 4:8–12; 13:23; Romans 10:9–13; Philippians 3:18–21.)

b. In light of these passages that point out how Jesus is Savior in a way Caesar was not, in what ways do the charges brought against Paul and Silas in Thessalonica begin to make sense?

4. In the Christian Text, Jesus is most commonly addressed and described as "Lord," and to most Romans, Caesar also was "Lord." So the implication that Caesar wasn't "Lord" was unavoidable. In fact, Paul frequently used "Lord" (*Kyrios* in Greek, *Adonai* in Hebrew) to declare Jesus' authority and right to reign. What impact do you think Ephesians 1:15–23 (particularly verses 18–21) had on the Jewish community? On followers of Jesus? On loyal Roman citizens and authorities?

DID YOU KNOW?
Honoring the Name of God

Paul used the title "Lord" (*Kyrios* in Greek, *Adonai* in Hebrew) for Jesus as a declaration of his authority or superior status that gave him the right to rule. This title was familiar to the Jewish community because they commonly used *Adonai* in place of God's sacred name: *YHWH*, which they did not use out of respect for God and fear of misrepresenting him. Hence, for the Jewish reader, Paul's use of the title "Lord" not only declared that Jesus had the authority to rule as King but implied he had that authority because he was the Son of God.

When God revealed his name to Moses, his response is generally translated "I am who I am" but can also be "I will be what I will be." In Hebrew, this is often written YHVH[17] and pronounced Yahweh. Both the meaning and pronunciation of this name are not entirely clear. The Hebrew letters for God's name are YHWH (vowels were pronounced but not written in ancient Hebrew), and they appear more than 6,800 times in the Hebrew Bible alone. Most scholars believe YHWH is related to a root word meaning "to be present" or "to exist" and probably meant either "he creates or causes" or simply "I am (that I am)," meaning that God did not depend on anyone or anything for his existence. This identification of God meant that his name could be used only of him and for him, because nothing else could possibly measure up to such a description.

For this reason, the Jewish people avoided using God's name. After all, who among God's creatures can truly understand the sovereign Creator of the universe? They did not want to use God's name in ways he had not revealed, so they chose to call him by other names such as "Lord" (*Adonai*), "God" (*Elohim*), "The Name" (*Ha-Shem*).

5. Perhaps the most significant description for Jesus is that he is not only *Lord* but *Christ*: the Lord's anointed one, meaning Jesus is *King*! The English word *Christ* comes from the Greek word *christos*, which means anointed, and the Hebrew word for anointed is *maschiach*, or "Messiah" in English. So both terms—Christ and Messiah—most often applied to a king chosen, equipped, and called to a mission by God. This identity would have been clearly understood by both Jews and Gentiles in the Roman world.[18]

   a. Throughout Israel's history, priests, prophets, and kings were anointed with oil to signify God's appointment to their mission. The phrases "anointed one," "the Lord's anointed," and "the Lord's Messiah" were commonly used in reference to kings. What sense do you get as to how significant and highly regarded God's anointed one was from Samuel's anointing of Saul (1 Samuel 10:1) and David (1 Samuel 16:10–13) and from David's behavior in 1 Samuel 24:1–10?

   b. As God's great plan of redemption is revealed through the Hebrew Bible, what promise does God make related to his anointed one, a descendant of David, and why would the fulfillment of that promise be threatening to other kingdoms? (See 1 Chronicles 17:11–24.)

    c. What insight does this understanding of the nature of God's anointed one—the king of the Jews, the Christ, Messiah—provide as to why King Herod responded to the birth of Jesus as he did? (See Matthew 2:1–8, 16.)

    d. How unsettling would the news and claims found in Luke 2:10–11 and 23:2 be to those in power in the first-century Roman world, and why?

Reflection

When Paul taught and explained the message of the gospel in the synagogue in Thessalonica and concluded, "This Jesus I am proclaiming to you is the Messiah,"[19] he rocked the Roman world to its core. Both those who believed Paul's message as well as those who didn't understood that if Jesus was Messiah, then he was the reigning King! For that they started a riot. Thessalonica, which had experienced the pain of disloyalty to Rome as well as the benefits of loyalty, had too much to lose to recognize any king other than Caesar.

The imperial cult, initiated by Caesar Augustus, the Caesar of Jesus' day, gave people of the Roman Empire an opportunity to demonstrate their loyalty to their ruler, lord, savior, and king. And they expended great effort to do so because of the favor it brought in the form of benefactions from Rome. King Herod the Great, for example, built three temples for the worship of Caesar Augustus in Israel. Even the public (and some private) events of everyday Roman life became opportunities to celebrate the worship of the emperor. The authorities of Thessalonica were not about to let the testimony of a foreigner, a Jew, undermine the gospel of Caesar with talk of a competing king. They were prepared to obey and defend their king and preserve his kingdom.

But what about those who believed that Jesus was Messiah, God's anointed King? They professed that Jesus was their King. They called him "Lord" to show that they were submitted to his reign. Were they, also, prepared to obey him and further his kingdom?

Calling Jesus "Lord" or "Christ" (anointed King) is more than a confession of belief and faith. Jesus said,

> *Not everyone who says to me, "Lord, Lord," will enter the kingdom of heaven, but only the one who does the will of my Father who is in heaven (Matthew 7:21).*

And again in Luke 6:46–49 he said,

> *Why do you call me, "Lord, Lord," and do not do what I say? As for everyone who comes to me and hears my words and puts them into practice, I will show you what they are like. They are like a man building a house, who dug down deep and laid the foundation on rock. When a flood came, the torrent struck that house but could not shake it, because it was well built. But the one who hears my words and does not put them into practice is like a man who built a house on the ground without a foundation. The moment the torrent struck that house, it collapsed and its destruction was complete.*

To call Jesus "Lord" or "Christ" means far more than a profession of belief or assent to a particular doctrine. It is to profess that Jesus has the authority to reign over us, which has profound implications for every part of life. And it is to submit to his reign by imitating his ways and walking in obedience to his commands.

Being subject to a king is not a concept we naturally understand, but we begin to grasp it as we learn the meaning of the language of the gospel. What new understanding of Jesus as Messiah, God's anointed one, will you walk in as a result of what you have learned today?

If you profess Jesus as Lord of your life, is he truly Lord of all of it? In which areas of life have you rejected his authority to be your Lord?

What in your life would change if you obeyed the gospel of our Lord Jesus with all your heart, soul, and strength?

Study Three | Conflict over the Gospel of Peace

The Very Words of God

Now may the Lord of peace himself give you peace at all times and in every way. The Lord be with all of you.

2 Thessalonians 3:16

Bible Discovery

Pax Romana vs. the Peace of God

Shalom is the peace of God that all humanity longs for. To the Hebrew understanding, *shalom* is the essence of who God is. It is the condition of creation before sin entered the world, when God saw that it was "very good." [20] It is the harmonious, abundant state of life overflowing with meaning, purpose, beauty, and wholeness—all without imperfection, exactly as God intended it to be. It is justice and life without hate, prejudice, envy, violence, disease, disaster, and death. It is the opposite of the chaos the kingdom of the Evil One has brought into the world.

Just as God brought *shalom* out of the formless and empty chaos when he created the world,[21] God's great plan of redemption, when the time is right for its fulfillment, will defeat chaos and restore God's kingdom and his peace to all creation. There will once again be harmony between God and his creation, God and humanity, and individual people. This coming kingdom where God's *shalom* will reign is presented and anticipated with hope throughout the Bible.

This is the peace of God that Paul proclaimed and offered to the Thessalonians if they believed in the Lord Jesus Christ. But as is true for nearly every truth of the gospel of Christ, the Thessalonians were already familiar with another kind of peace: the peace of the gospel of Caesar and the Roman Empire. That peace came by the spear and slashing sword of the Roman legions. It was a peace that promised (and, for some, delivered) security and prosperity, but it also assured the annihilation of all who resisted it. There are subtle clues that even people who were loyal to Rome realized that *Pax Romana* did not satisfy their deepest longing for peace. The philosopher Epictetus, for example, wrote:

> For you see that Caesar appears to furnish us with great peace, that there are no longer enemies nor battles nor great associations of robbers nor of pirates, but we can travel at every hour and sail from east to west. But can Caesar give us security from fever also, can he from shipwreck, from fire, from earthquake or from lightning? Well, I will say, can he give us security against love? He cannot. From sorrow? He cannot. From envy? He cannot. In a word then he cannot protect us from any of these things.[22]

Paul knew that *shalom*, the true peace of God that satisfies the deep longings of the human heart comes only through Jesus and the reign of his kingdom. That peace is inherent to the gospel of Christ that Paul brought to the Roman world. When Paul proclaimed the peace that comes through the Lord Jesus, what would the people of Thessalonica hear in his words and how would they respond?

1. God's promise of a future kingdom of peace, or *shalom*, is woven throughout the Hebrew Text. According to Isaiah 52:7, a passage we have considered several times during this study, what announcement is inherent in the gospel message—the good news—that Jesus Christ brings salvation to his people?

2. When we think of who Jesus is and what he has done for us, we often think in terms of love, forgiveness, salvation, and sacrifice, but *shalom* may not be near the top of our list. Yet God's peace is a reality that comes from Jesus and his redemptive work; it is part of the gospel message he came to teach, demonstrate, and pass on to his disciples. *Shalom* was evident in every part of his life.

    a. What was announced on earth when Jesus was born? (See Luke 2:13–14.)

    b. When we think of Jesus' miracles, we often focus on what happened, but what result did his miracles bring? (See Mark 4:39 [ESV]; Mark 5:33–34; Luke 7:50.)

c. What does Jesus offer to everyone who follows him, and what did he say was different about it? (See John 14:27; 16:33.)

d. What did Peter explain about how Jesus demonstrated the good news of peace he brought to the people of Israel? (See Acts 10:36–38.)

THINK ABOUT IT
The Pax Romana—The Roman Style of Peace
The peace Caesar Augustus achieved in the Roman Empire was such an unbelievable accomplishment that people were certain it proved his divinity. The world had never known such peace—no Roman civil wars, no threats from other empires—so how could Caesar be anything but divine?

Not only had Caesar Augustus brought an end to war, he subjugated the world to be used for Roman benefit. The wealthy and powerful benefitted greatly from the economic prosperity, leisure time, and pleasure that the peace of Caesar, lord and savior of the world, had delivered. Furthermore, Caesar declared the *Pax Romana* to be a gift from the gods. So he revived the worship of traditional Roman gods among the Roman people (and instituted it in conquered territories) by reforming the priesthood, restoring 82 temples, and building new temples—some dedicated to the worship of his family members or himself.

Certainly, Caesar Augustus brought a kind of peace to the Roman Empire. But is peace wrought by violence, death, and oppression through military conquest and brutal enforcement of law really peace? Might there be a peace that runs deeper than reprieve from military conflict and offers more than economic prosperity and personal pleasure?

THIS ALTAR, FOUND IN ITALY ABOUT TWENTY MILES EAST OF ROME, HONORS THE PROMISE CAESAR AUGUSTUS MADE TO BRING PEACE AND SECURITY TO THE ROMAN EMPIRE. ONE SIDE READS, "SACRED AUGUSTAN SECURITY," THE OTHER, "SACRED AUGUSTAN PEACE."

3. Paul understood that everything Jesus did, and the mission to which he called his followers, was to proclaim and demonstrate the gospel of peace. Peace is the gift promised to anyone who believes, and Paul frequently reminded believers of this amazing truth. What do the following passages reveal about Paul's understanding of this peace and its relationship to the gospel message? (See 1 Corinthians 7:15; Galatians 5:22–23; Ephesians 6:10–11, 15; 1 Thessalonians 1:1; 2 Thessalonians 1:2; 3:16.)

4. The peace of the gospel of Caesar came through violence and was preserved by fear of violence. In contrast, how does the peace of God's kingdom come to us? (See Colossians 1:20.)

    What does the peace of God offer that the peace of Rome can never offer? (See Philippians 4:4–7.)

    What are the risks of any peace that comes by way of Caesar's gospel? (See Isaiah 48:22; 1 Thessalonians 5:3.)

DID YOU KNOW?
Pilate Declared Jesus Innocent

Even during the "golden age" of *Pax Romana* there was an undercurrent of conflict, violence, and fear throughout Caesar's kingdom; quite a contrast to the *shalom* of the gospel of Jesus Christ that Paul proclaimed. It is fascinating to see how these two gospels interacted during the trial of Jesus before Pilate.[23]

As the Roman governor, Pilate knew the source of Roman peace and how it was maintained. He knew how important it was for him to determine if this self-proclaimed Jewish king was a threat to Roman peace. When Jesus said that his kingdom was "not of this world" and was "from another place," Pilate was relieved. Apparently, Jesus was no threat to *Pax Romana*, at least not by the violence Pilate was concerned about. So he declared Jesus to be innocent![24]

Ironically, the peace of the kingdom of heaven would come through the brutal crucifixion to which Pilate eventually sentenced Jesus. By sacrificing himself when he could have summoned legions of angels to save him, Jesus produced a far greater peace that continues to grow to this day and will last forever. Today, *Pax Romana* is no more. Tourists visit the ruins of its past. But the peace Paul brought to the Roman world lives on.

Reflection

The Thessalonians looked to their savior, Caesar, to solve their problems, satisfy their appetites, rescue them from trouble, deliver them from danger, protect their wealth from others, and make them happy. But though Caesar could bring an end to wars, unify people through worship of Roman gods (and himself as their emperor, of course), and apply the resources of an empire to make the material aspects of life easier and more pleasurable for his loyal subjects, he was powerless to bring the peace they truly desired.

Then Paul came, bringing the good news of Jesus, God's anointed King, the Savior and Lord who sacrificed himself in order to give the gift of *shalom* to all who would accept it. This message of peace offered freely to everyone stood in stark contrast to the gospel of Caesar. The announcement of another king—Jesus—whose authority and power surpasses that of all other kingdoms made the official enforcers of *Pax Romana* nervous and afraid. But the Thessalonian Christians did not fear the kingdom of Rome. They lived under the authority of Jesus and, in submission to his commands, did not keep that gospel to themselves.

The Thessalonian believers lived, as Paul had taught them, in a way that demonstrated *shalom* to their world. One person, one situation, one city block at a time they extended the peace of the kingdom of heaven to that pagan city. Yes, it caused a riot. Satan does not give up his kingdom without a fight. That's why God's partners—saved by grace, empowered by his Spirit, directed by his Word, and encouraged by his community—put on the armor of God and carry the sword of his Word.

Are you "in"? Are you part of the greatest thing God has done since creation? Then demonstrate God's reign in your life by proclaiming through your words and deeds his gospel of peace. Invite others to know the peace that comes when we are submitted to our Lord. When followers of Jesus do this, God's kingdom will come whether Caesar wants it to or not!

Paul instructed Jesus' followers in Thessalonica how to live in a way that demonstrated *shalom*, the peace of God. Read each of the following passages in light of the peace (life as God intended it) that people long to experience. Then write down specific ways you can demonstrate the peace of God in your world.

Do not wrong or take advantage of a brother or sister
(1 Thessalonians 4:6)

Love each other (1 Thessalonians 4:9)

Work in such a way that you earn the respect of others
(1 Thessalonians 4:11–12)

Encourage and build up one another (1 Thessalonians 5:11)

Live in peace with each other (1 Thessalonians 5:13)

Encourage the disheartened, help the weak, and be patient
with everyone (1 Thessalonians 5:14)

Don't repay evil for evil but do good to benefit everyone
(1 Thessalonians 5:15)

NOTES

Introduction

1. 1 Corinthians 12.

2. Sandra L. Richter, *The Epic of Eden* (Downers Grove, Ill.: InterVarsity Press, 2008), Chapter 1; Kenneth E. Bailey, *Jacob and the Prodigal* (Downers Grove, Ill.: InterVarsity Press, 2003), Chapter I, sections 1 and 3. These each provide an excellent description of the need to understand and properly use the cultural setting of the Bible.

3. Acts 6:5; 13:43; Romans 16:5; 1 Corinthians 16:15.

4. As we will discover, the word *gospel*, or *evangelion* in Greek, was a formal term for an official pronouncement about the divine emperor.

5. Acts 15:36–16:4, 10. Paul chose Silas (the shortened version of Sylvanus) and Timothy to join him. In Acts 16:10 Luke the author switches from "they" to describe Paul's work to "we," an indication that Luke joined them before they reached Philippi.

6. Philippians 1:2: "Grace and peace to you from God our Father and the Lord Jesus Christ."

7. John 17:6.

8. 1 Corinthians 11:1.

9. Matthew 5:14–16; 1 Peter 2:9–12.

10. 1 Corinthians 3:9.

11. Jeremiah 29:4–7.

12. Jonathon Sacks, in a speech entitled "The Western World and the JudeoChristian Revelation of God," presents a powerful vision of God working through his people who

have little power or influence on their own. I find this idea compelling, given how tempting it is to seek to bring God's will by economic or political power rather than by faithful living.

13. Acts 23:6.

14. Acts 22:3.

15. Philippians 3:5; Acts 23:6.

16. Philippians 1:14.

17. Philippians 1:27.

Timeline

1. Not all scholars agree on some dates in the life of Paul. One of the most helpful timelines is found in Ben Witherington, *The Acts of the Apostles: A Socio-Rhetorical Commentary* (Grand Rapids: Eerdmans, 1998), 81–86.

2. According to the writings of St. Jerome, the great Church Father (342–420 AD), Saul's parents were originally from Gischala in northern Galilee. They apparently joined in a revolt against Rome and were exiled to Tarsus as slaves. Although this tradition is unsupported, Jerome is considered a reliable source. The Romans exiled Jewish slaves from northern Galilee in 61, 55, 52, and 4 BC and 6 AD. Saul's parents then would have been freed from slavery—made "freedmen"—in order for Saul to be born a Roman citizen. See also Bargil Pixner, *The Fifth Gospel: With Jesus Through Galilee* (Rosh Pina, Israel: Corazin Publishing, 1992), 76.

3. This was apparently a "rabbi-disciple" relationship as the text (NRSV) literally says, "brought up in this city at the feet of Gamaliel," which is the Jewish phrase used for such training. While it is impossible to assign exact dates for this study, a boy usually began rabbinic training at about age twelve (6 AD) and studied until he was thirty (30 AD).

4. Luke's account in Acts ends with Paul in prison in Rome. However, church tradition holds that Paul was released after his first imprisonment and continued to teach the good news of Jesus. Events after his imprisonment are inferred by hints in Paul's pastoral letters (see Romans 15:28). It is likely Paul was arrested again and executed during Nero's persecution.

Session 1: The Gospel of Caesar

1. Habakkuk 2:14.

2. Acts 16:12 refers to Philippi as a Roman colony.

3. I credit Lois Tverberg for her unpublished research pointing out the connection between Paul's writings and the Isaiah passages.

4. Diodorus Siculus, *The Reign of Philip II: The Greek and Macedonian Narrative*, from Book XVI, trans. E. J. McQueen, Bristol Classical Press.

5. For an in-depth study of Paul's first teaching journey, please see That the World May Know, Vol. 7, *Walk as Jesus Walked*, sessions 1, 2, 3.

6. For an in-depth study of Paul's third teaching tour, please see That the World May Know, Vol. 5, *Early Church*, sessions 2, 3, 4, 5.

7. Readily available on the internet: *The Acts of Divine Augustus*, or in Latin, *Res Gestae Divi Augusti*.

8. Tacitus, *Agricola* 30, readily available on the internet.

9. Psalm 14:1–3; 53:1–3; Ecclesiastes 7:20.

10. Psalm 5:9.

11. Psalm 140:3.

12. Psalm 10:7 (see Septuagint).

13. Isaiah 59:7–8.

14. Psalm 36:1.

Session 2: The Believers

1. See Isaiah 52:7.

2. See Acts 22:1–5; 26:4–5; Philippians 3:5–6.

3. Philippians 1:6.

4. Jewish burial inscription uncovered in recent excavations of the western necropolis in Philippi, according to personal communication with the director of the Museum of Philippi.

5. Josephus, *Antiquities*, 12.138 ff. See Josephus, *Josephus: Complete Works*, trans. William Whiston (1867) reprint (Grand Rapids: Kregel, 1972).

6. Josephus, *Antiquities*, 10.14.25. See Josephus, *Josephus: Complete Works*.

7. Ancient writer Dio Cassius, *Divus Claudius*, no. 25.

8. Pischa Mekhilta, 1:64–65. See S. Safrai and M. Stern, *The Jewish People in the First Century* (Amsterdam: Van Gorcum, 1976), 938. Lois Tverberg, PhD, pointed out this source and connection.

9. For further study of *mikveh* in Jewish tradition, please see That the World May Know, Vol. 3, *Life and Ministry of the Messiah*, session 3, and Vol. 11, *The Path to the Cross*, sessions 1 and 2.

10. For further discussion of Paul's early preparation, see That the World May Know, Vol. 7, *Walk as Jesus Walked*, session 2.

11. The Bible uses different Greek words having basically the same meaning: *Phoboumenos ton Theon and Seboumenos ton Theon* which mean the same as the title on the pillar: "God-fearing person." See J. Reynolds and R. Tannenbaum, *Jews and God-fearers at Aphrodisias: Greek Inscriptions with Commentary*, Proceedings of the Cambridge Philological Association, Supp.12 (Cambridge: Cambridge Philological Society, 1987).

12. Ben Witherington, *The Acts of the Apostles: A Socio-Rhetorical Commentary* (Grand Rapids: Eerdmans, 1998), 493ff.

13. See Sandra Richter, *Epic of Eden* (Downers Grove, Ill.: InterVarsity Press, 2008), see chapter 1. I find this book most helpful in understanding the broad context of Scripture. Her chapter on the meaning of redemption in a tribal society is superb.

14. See Numbers 22–25. Moab acted to prevent Israel from reaching the Promised Land and enticed the Hebrews to sin, bringing God's anger against them. In response, God prohibited Moab from joining the community of his people. Apparently, God made an exception for Ruth due to her commitment to join his people.

15. Acts 16:12.

16. James S. Jeffers, *The Greco-Roman World of the New Testament Era* (Downers Grove, Ill.: InterVarsity Press, 1999), 209.

17. Romans were not monotheists. While everyone worshiped the emperor, it was common to also worship a primary god along with several others. If household conversions meant renouncing all gods but the Lord, the households of believers would have been quite unique from their neighbors, creating a great opportunity to put God on display.

Session 3: The Powers of Darkness

1. James S. Jeffers, *The Greco-Roman World of the New Testament Era* (Downers Grove, Ill.: InterVarsity Press, 1999), see chapter 11. Also, Roland Worth, *The Seven Cities of the Apocalypse and Roman Culture* (New York: Paulist Press, 1999), 36ff.

2. W. V. Harris, "Trade" in *Cambridge Ancient History: The High Empire AD 70–192* (Cambridge: Cambridge University Press, 2000), vol. 11, 721. Caesar Augustus, emperor at Jesus' birth, imposed a 2 percent sales tax on the sale of slaves that produced the equivalent of $6 million annual income. Based on the average price of a slave, that would be approximately 250,000 slave transactions per year.

3. Adolf Deissmann, *Light from the Ancient Near East* (New York: Hodder and Stoughton, 1910).

4. John MacArthur, *Slave: The Hidden Truth About Your Identity in Christ* (Nashville: Thomas Nelson, 2010), 15.

5. Doug Greewold, "Reclaiming Our Identity in Christ: The High Calling of Being a Slave of Christ," *Preserving Bible Times*, Reflection no. 914, 2014. An excellent essay on being a "slave" of Christ. www.preservingbibletimes.org. I credit Greewold for pointing out the contrasts between a servant and a slave.

6. "Ancient Life: Childhood's End," *Archaeology Odyssey*, July/August 2003, vol. 6, no. 4. http://members.bibarch.org/search.asp?PubID=BSAO&Volume=6&Issue=4&ArticleID=11&UserID=0&

7. Hilary LeCornu, *The Jewish Roots of Acts,* Vol. 2 (Jerusalem: Academon Jerusalem, 2003), 891. Luke used the word *paidiske* to describe another young slave girl named Rhoda. She answered the door of the house where Peter went to join the other disciples after God miraculously freed him from Herod Agrippa. See also Matthew 26:69; Mark 14:66; Luke 22:56 (Note: The English word *servant* is commonly used even when *slave* would be the more literal translation.)

8. Quoted in Edwin Yamauchi, *Harper's World of the New Testament* (San Francisco: Harper and Row, 1981), 94.

9. I thank Lois Tverberg, PhD, for some of these insights.

10. See Matthew 12:22–29. For further study, see That the World May Know, Vol. 14, *The Mission of Jesus*, sessions 1 and 2.

11. Please note that the Greek word *doulos* is translated as *servant* in this verse rather than as *slave*. *Slave* would better represent how people of that time understood the word.

12. For an in-depth study of the role of oracles in the Greek and Roman world, please see That the World May Know, Vol. 6, *In the Dust of the Rabbi*, session 5.

13. See "Was She Really Stoned?" *Archaeology Odyssey*, November/December 2002.

14. Ben Witherington, *The Acts of the Apostles: A Socio-Rhetorical Commentary* (Grand Rapids: Eerdmans, 1998), 495.

15. For an in-depth study of Jesus binding the Evil One, please see That the World May Know, Vol. 14, *The Mission of Jesus*, sessions 1 and 2.

Session 4: The Philippian Jailer

1. Acts 2.

2. For further study on distinctive Jewish dress and the wearing of tassels, please see That the World May Know, Vol. 13, *Israel's Mission: Becoming a Kingdom of Priests in a Prodigal World*, session 2.

3. Bargil Pixner, *With Jesus Through Galilee According to the Fifth Gospel* (Rosh Pina, Israel: Corazin Publishing, 1992), 76.

4. Brian Rapske, *The Book of Acts in the First Century Setting, Paul in Roman Custody*, vol. 3 (Grand Rapids: Eerdmans, 1994), 131.

5. Victor Ko, cited in an article in *The Banner: The Magazine of the Christian Reformed Church* 151, no 8 (September 2016): 19.

6. Christian History for Everyman, www.christian-history.org. Although further identity of the writer and the recipient of the letter is uncertain, the Epistle, consisting of twelve chapters, is generally dated between 130–200 AD.

7. See Numbers 15:37–41; Deuteronomy 22:12.

8. See En-Gedi Resource Center, http://www.egrc.net, "Director's Article," June 2003, and "Biblical Dress: Tassels." See the Jewish Publication Society Commentary on Numbers, by Jacob Milgrom, 1990, excursus 38 on tassels (*Tsitsit*). See also That the World May Know, Vol. 3, *Life and Ministry of the Messiah*, session 5.

9. Suetonius, *Life of Claudius*, 25.4. Available in several translations on the internet. See also Acts 18:2.

10. Rapske, *The Book of Acts in Its First Century Setting, Paul in Roman Custody*, chapter 5.

11. Hillary LeCornu and Joseph Shulam, *A Commentary on the Jewish Roots of Acts*, vol. 2 (Jerusalem: Academon, 2003), 903.

12. Rapske, *The Book of Acts in Its First Century Setting, Paul in Roman Custody*, chapter 5.

13. On different occasions I have shared this story with two orthodox Jewish scholars. Although both of them were unfamiliar with this account of Paul's life, both immediately referred to this psalm of David and also mentioned the evening recitation of the *shema*.

14. Dr. Kosta Kolizeras was a fantastic scholar and teacher who passed away in 2016. I have never personally met anyone more knowledgeable about Greek and Roman history and archaeology or able to use that knowledge so well to better understand the Bible. I am grateful for his insights and contributions to this study series on Greece and Rome.

15. Ben Witherington, *The Acts of the Apostles: A Socio-Rhetorical Commentary* (Grand Rapids: Eerdmans, 1998), 497.

16. Octavian, who later took the title Caesar Augustus, applied this law when he avenged the assassination of Julius Caesar, his father. He "proscribed" more than 200 of his enemies, meaning they lost their citizenship and legal protection. This public condemnation declared the person to be an enemy of the state and worthy of execution. Anyone who executed the "proscribed" person was entitled to part of his estate, and the remainder went to the state. None of the estate would pass to the "proscribed" person's family.

17. LeCornu and Shulam, *A Commentary on the Jewish Roots of Acts*, vol. 2, 910.

18. Witherington, *The Acts of the Apostles: A Socio-Rhetorical Commentary*, 501.

Session 5: Confronting the Empire

1. Romans 1:5; 16:26.

2. Philippians 2:15; 1 Thessalonians 4:11–12; Titus 2:9–10.

3. Ephesians 2:19–22.

4. Galatians 1:13–14.

5. Acts 5:34–40.

6. Romans 15:9–10.

7. Daniel 3:28–29.

8. Acts 18:2.

9. For an excellent explanation of this idea, see Ben Witherington, *The Acts of the Apostles; A Socio-Rhetorical Commentary* (Grand Rapids: Eerdmans, 1998), 504–505.

10. Acts 17:3–5.

11. John 11:45–48.

12. For further study on Paul's early preparation for his mission, see That the World May Know, Vol. 7, *Walk as Jesus Walked*, session 2, 70ff.

13. Ruth 1:15–17.

14. Gene L. Green, *Letters to the Thessalonians*, The Pillar New Testament Commentary (Grand Rapids: Eerdmans, 2002), 50. Ben Witherington, *The Acts of the Apostles: A Socio-Rhetorical Commentary* (Grand Rapids: Eerdmans, 1998), 508. See 1 Thessalonians 1:1; 2 Thessalonians 2:1.

15. A Greek term *oikoumene* meaning "inhabited earth," often found on inscriptions and coins to describe those who had received Caesar's benefits and were loyal to him. It meant "the whole world." It is also a term used several times in the Scripture both to describe those who opposed Jesus and those over whom he was Lord (Revelation 3:10; 6:10; 11:10; 13:8, 12, 14; 14:6; 17:12).

16. Craig Evans, "Mark's Incipit and the Priene Calendar Inscription: From Jewish Gospel to Greco-Roman Gospel," *Journal of Greco-Roman Christianity and Judaism*, 1 (2000): 68–69,

who footnotes his source as M. E. Boring, K. Berger, and C. Colpe, *Hellenistic Commentary to the New Testament* (Nashville: Abingdon, 1995).

17. In Hebrew it is spelled *yod-heh-vav-heh* with the *vav* pronounced as a *w*.

18. I am grateful for the contribution of Lois Tverberg's understanding of these concepts presented in her article "Believe in Christ: It's Not What You Think" on her blogsite, Our Rabbi Jesus.

19. Acts 17:3.

20. Genesis 1:31.

21. Genesis 1:1–2.

22. Epictetus, *The Discourses*, 3.13.9–10.

23. John 18:29–19:22. The conflict between the gospels of Caesar and Jesus is also evident in the emphasis of the Jewish leaders on the claims of Jesus to be the "Son of God" and their claim that they had no king but Caesar!

24. John 18:38; 19:4.

ACKNOWLEDGMENTS

The production of this study series is the work of a community of people. Many contributed their time and talent to make it possible. Recognizing the work of that unseen community is to me an important confirmation that we have learned the lessons God has been teaching his people for more than three thousand years. Here are the people God has used to make this study possible.

The Prince Foundation:

The vision of Elsa and Ed Prince—that this project that began in 1993 would enable thousands of people around the world to walk in the footsteps of the people of God—has never waned. God continues to use Elsa's commitment to share God's story with our broken world.

Focus on the Family:

Bob DeMoss—vice president, content development

Mitchell Wright—executive producer, visual media

Erin Berriman—lead coordinating producer, visual media

Paul Murphy—manager, video post-production

Blain Andersen—video editor

Christi Lynn—director, product marketing

Allison Montjoy—manager, product marketing

Kay Leavy—senior coordinator, resource marketing

Larry Weeden—director, book and curriculum development and acquisition

Zondervan:

John Raymond—vice president and publisher, curriculum

Beth Murphy—senior director, curriculum marketing and sales

T. J. Rathbun—director, audio/visual production

Tammy Johnson—art director

Ben Fetterley, Denise Froehlich—book interior designers

Greg Clouse—production editor

That the World May Know:

Chris Hayden—research assistant. This series would not have been completed nor would it have the excellence of content it has without his outstanding research effort.

Lois Tverberg, PhD

Nadav Hillebrand

Alison Elders

Lisa Fredicks

Grooters Productions:

John Grooters—producer/director

Judy Grooters—producer

Mark Chamberlin—director of photography

Mark Chamberlin, John Grooters, Adam Vardy, Tyler Jackson—cinematography

Kent Esmeier—online editor/colorist

Alan Arroyo—assistant editor

Paul Wesselink—re-recording mixer and sound design

Christian Nikkel, Aleece Cook—additional sound

Carlos Martinez—orchestrations

Brittany Grooters, Jordyn Osburn, Hannah Dozeman, Hollie Noble—post-production assistants

Dave Lassanske, Shawn Kamerman, Eric Schrotenboer, Kate Chamberlin—camera assistants

Paul Wesselink, Ryan Wert—production sound

Dennis Lassanske, Alan Arroyo, Brittany Grooters, Taylor Wogomon, Hannah Dozeman, Nola Tolsma—production support

Taylor Wogoman, Dave Lassanske—motion graphics

Breana Melvin, Charlie Shaw, Rob Perry, John Walker, Drew Johnson—illustrators

Eric Schrotenboer—music

Sorenson Communications:

Stephen and Amanda Sorenson—writers

BIBLIOGRAPHY

Bailey, Kenneth E. *Jacob and the Prodigal*. Downers Grove, Ill.: IVP Academic, 2003.

_____. *Paul Through Mediterranean Eyes*. Downers Grove, Ill.: IVP Academic, 2008.

Bauckham, Richard, ed. *The Book of Acts in Its Palestinian Setting*, vol. 4. Grand Rapids: Eerdmans, 1995.

Bayram, Tekin, ed. *First International Congress on Antioch of Pisidia: A Collection of Scholarly Papers*. Yalvac, Turkey: Kocaeli Publishers, 1997.

Beitzel, Barry J. *Moody Bible Atlas*. Chicago: Moody Press, 1985.

Berlin, Adele, and Mark Zvi Brettler. *Jewish Study Bible*. Philadelphia: Jewish Publication Society and New York: Oxford University Press, 2004.

Bivin, David. *New Light on the Difficult Words of Jesus: Insights from His Jewish Context*. Holland, Mich.: EnGedi Resource Center, 2005. (www.egrc.net)

Crossan, John Dominic and Jonathon L. Reed. *In Search of Paul*. San Francisco: Harper, 2004.

Danby, Herbert. *The Mishnah*. New York: Oxford University Press, 1977, Sanhedrin 4.5.

Evans, Craig A. "Mark's Incipit and the Priene Calendar Inscription: From Jewish Gospel to Greco-Roman Gospel" *Journal of Greco-Roman Christianity and Judaism* 1 (2000), 67–81. (http://www.craigaevans.com/studies.htm)

Fitzmyer, Joseph A. *The Acts of the Apostles*, The Anchor Bible Commentary. New York: Doubleday, 1998.

Garnsey, Peter. *Social Status and Legal Privilege in the Roman Empire*. Clarendon, England: Oxford Press, 1970.

Gill, David W. J., and Conrad Gempf. *The Book of Acts in Its First Century Setting: Graeco-Roman Setting*, vol. 2. Grand Rapids: Eerdmans, 1994.

Green, Gene L. *Letters to the Thessalonians*. The Pillar New Testament Commentary. Grand Rapids: Eerdmans, 2002.

Gundry, Robert H. *Mark: A Commentary on His Apology for the Cross*. Grand Rapids: Eerdmans Publishing, 1993.

Hansen, G. Walter. *The Letter to the Philippians.* Pillar New Testament Commentary. Grand Rapids: Eerdmans, 2009.

Hengel, Martin. *Crucifixion in the Ancient World and the Folly of the Message of the Cross.* Philadelphia: Fortress, 1977.

Hillers, Delbert R. *Covenant: The History of a Biblical Idea.* Baltimore: Johns Hopkins Press, 1969.

Howard-Brook, Wes. *Come Out My People!* Maryknoll, N.Y.: Orbis Books, 2011.

Jeffers, James S. *The Greco-Roman World of the New Testament Era.* Downers Grove, Ill.: IVP Academic, 1999.

LeCornu, Hilary. *The Jewish Roots of Acts,* vols. 1 and 2. Jerusalem: Academon, 2003.

Levinskaya, Irina. *The Book of Acts in Its First Century Setting: Diaspora Setting,* vol. 5. Grand Rapids: Eerdmans, 1994.

Meeks, Wayne. *The First Urban Christians: The Social World of the Apostle Paul.* New Haven: Yale University Press, 1983.

Notley, Steven R. and Ze'ev Safrai. *Parables of the Sages.* Jerusalem: Carta, 2011.

Pixner, Bargil. *With Jesus Through Galilee According to the Fifth Gospel.* Rosh Pina, Israel: Corazin Publishing, 1992.

Pryor, Dwight A. *Unveiling the Kingdom of Heaven.* Dayton, Ohio: Center for Judaic Christian Studies, 2008. (www.jcstudies.com)

Rainey, Anson F. and R. Steven Notley. *The Sacred Bridge: Carta's Atlas of the Biblical World.* Jerusalem: Carta, 2007, page 360.

Rapske, Brian. *The Book of Acts in Its First Century Setting: Paul in Roman Custody,* vol. 3. Grand Rapids: Eerdmans, 1994.

Richter, Sandra L. *The Epic of Eden.* Downers Grove, Ill.: IVP Academic, 2008.

Ryken, Leland, James C. Wilhoit, and Tremper Longman III. *Dictionary of Biblical Imagery.* Downers Grove, Ill.: IVP Academic, 1998.

Safrai, S. and M. Stern. *The Jewish People in the First Century.* Amsterdam: Van Gorcum, 1976.

Santala, Risto. *Paul: The Man and the Teacher.* Jerusalem: Keren Ahvah Meshihit, 1995.

Taylor, Lily Ross. *The Divinity of the Emperor.* Middletown, Conn.: Scholars Press, 1931.

Telushkin, Rabbi Joseph. *The Book of Jewish Values.* New York: Bell Tower Publishers, 2000, page 70.

Tverberg, Lois. *Walking in the Dust of Rabbi Jesus*. Grand Rapids: Zondervan, 2012.

Tverberg, Lois, with Bruce Okkema. *Listening to the Language of the Bible*. Holland, Mich.: En Gedi Resource Center, 2004. (www.egrc.net)

Tverberg, Lois and Ann Spangler. *Sitting at the Feet of Rabbi Jesus*. Grand Rapids: Zondervan, 2009.

Weima, Jeffrey. *1–2 Thessalonians*. Baker Exegetical Commentary. Grand Rapids: Baker Academic, 2014.

Whiston, William, trans. *Flavius Josephus: The Jewish War. VII. 3–7*. Complete works of Josephus.

_____. *Josephus: Complete Works, Antiquities*, 10.14.25. See Josephus, *Josephus: Complete Works* (1867). Reprint. Grand Rapids: Kregel, 1971.

White, Michael I. *Building God's House in the Roman World*. Baltimore: Johns Hopkins University, 1990.

Wilson, Mark. "In the Footsteps of Paul in Asia Minor: Are There Still Roman Roads Left to Follow?" *Biblical Archaeology Society Lecture Series*, Fest XII—Part 2. Washington, D.C., 2010.

Wilson, Marvin R. *Exploring our Hebraic Heritage*. Grand Rapids: Eerdmans, 2014.

Witherington, Ben. *Friendship and Finances in Philippi*. Valley Forge, Pa.: Trinity Press International, 1994.

_____. *New Testament History*. Grand Rapids: Baker, 2001.

_____. *The Acts of the Apostles*. Grand Rapids: Eerdmans, 1998.

_____. *The Acts of the Apostles: A Socio-Rhetorical Commentary*. Grand Rapids: Eerdmans, 1998.

Worth, Roland H. *The Seven Cities of the Apocalypse and Roman Culture*. New York: Paulist Press, 1999.

Wright, Christopher J. H. *The Mission of God*. Downers Grove, Ill.: IVP Academic, 2006.

Wright, N. T. "Paul, Arabia, and Elijah: Galatians 1:17." *Journal of Biblical Literature*, vol. 115, 683–692.

_____. *Simply Jesus: A New Vision of Who He Was, What He Did, and Why He Matters*. New York: Harper Collins, 2011.

Yamauchi, Edwin. *Harper's World of the New Testament*. San Francisco: Harper and Row, 1981.

Young, Brad H. *The Parables: Jewish Tradition and Christian Interpretation*. Peabody, Mass.: Hendrickson Publishers, 1998.

More Great Resources
from Focus on the Family®

Volume 1: Promised Land
This volume focuses on the Old Testament—particularly on the nation of ancient Israel, God's purpose for His people, and why He placed them in the Promised Land.

Volume 2: Prophets and Kings
This volume looks into the nation of Israel during Old Testament times to understand how the people struggled with the call of God to be a separate and holy nation.

Volume 3: Life and Ministry of the Messiah
This volume explores the life and teaching ministry of Jesus. Discover new insights about the Son of God.

Volume 4: Death and Resurrection of the Messiah
Witness the passion of the Messiah as He resolutely sets His face toward Jerusalem to suffer and die for His bride. Discover the thrill the disciples felt when they learned of His resurrection and were later filled with the Holy Spirit.

Volume 5: The Early Church
Capture the fire of the early church in this fifth set of That the World May Know® film series. See how the first Christians lived out their faith with a passion that literally changed the world.

Volume 6: In the Dust of the Rabbi
"Follow the rabbi, drink in his words, and be covered with the dust of his feet," says the ancient Jewish proverb. Come discover how to follow Jesus as you walk with teacher and historian Ray Vander Laan through the breathtaking terrains of Israel and Turkey and explore what it really means to be a disciple.

Volume 7: Walk as Jesus Walked
Journey to Israel where the 12 disciples walked the walk their rabbi Jesus taught them. Examining the culture and the politics of the first century, Ray Vander Laan opens up the Gospels as never before.

Volume 8: God Heard Their Cry
Just when it seemed that Pharaoh could not be defeated, God provided for His people in ways they never could have imagined. Join historian Ray Vander Laan in ancient Egypt for his study of God's faithfulness to the Israelites—a promise that remains true today.

Volume 9: Fire on the Mountain

When the Israelites left Egypt, they were finally free. But with that freedom comes a new challenge—learning how to live together the way God intends. Discover how God teaches the Israelites (and us) what it means to be part of a community that loves Him.

Volume 10: With All Your Heart

In this volume, you'll learn how quickly the Israelites forgot God after they entered the Promised Land. Do you remember where your blessings come from?

Volume 11: The Path to the Cross

Discover how the Israelites' passionate faith prepares the way for Jesus, and be challenged to live as they did—by every word that comes from the mouth of God.

Volume 12: Walking with God in the Desert

Are you going through a difficult period of life? During these desert times, it's easy to think God has disappeared. Instead, discover that it's only when we're totally dependent on God that we find Him closer than ever.

Volume 13: Israel's Mission

God gave the assignment to His people thousands of years ago: to bring "lost sheep" back into His kingdom. And it's still our task today. Glimpse the urgency and rewards of welcoming the strangers and prodigals the Lord longs to embrace. Discover the mission that can give your life greater meaning than you ever imagined.

Volume 14: The Mission of Jesus

In John 17:26 Jesus says: "I made known your name to them, and I will continue to make it known." In this volume, you'll deepen your understanding of this passionate revelation to a broken world God longs to redeem. Discover how Jesus triumphantly made God's presence known on Earth, and how he asks you to do the same—bringing God's shalom to those in chaos.

FOCUS ON THE FAMILY®

Online: Go to ThatTheWorldMayKnow.com

Phone: Call toll-free: 800-A-FAMILY (232-6459)

In Canada, call toll-free: 800-661-9800